Praise for *Talking with Dogs and Cats and* ...

"This wonderful book is filled with so much invaluable information about truly communicating with our dear animals. I loved it!"
— Alison Pace, author of *You Tell Your Dog First*

"Communication is everything! Tim Link's wonderfully informative book gives us the tools we need for understanding our pets' wants and needs using a language they understand."
— Sue Chipperton, coauthor of *A Famous Dog's Life: The Story of Gidget, America's Most Beloved Chihuahua*

"Tim Link is the best friend any dog or cat ever had — providing an insightful, heartwarming guide to teaching us what our pets are truly thinking and feeling. The more you read it, the stronger the connection between you and man's best friend will be."
— Glenn Plaskin, bestselling author of *Katie Up and Down the Hall: The True Story of How One Dog Turned Five Neighbors into a Family*

"Tim Link does the impossible by taking the mystery out of communicating with dogs and cats. He combines excellent training tips with compassionate and respectful conversations about separation anxiety, behavior issues, changes in routine, and new additions to the family. Anyone can use Link's methods. If everyone did, fewer animals would lose their homes. Give this insightful and necessary book to anyone with a pet."
— Allen and Linda Anderson, *New York Times*–bestselling authors of *A Dog Named Leaf*, *Angel Dogs*, and *Angel Cats* and founders of Angel Animals Network

"Most of us have an intuitive sense that our dogs and cats understand a great deal of our verbal and nonverbal communication. In this informative work, Tim Link digs deeper into the phenomenon and helps us to better communicate with our pets. Highly recommended for anyone who wants to enhance their relationships with their pets."

— Greg Kincaid, author of *A Dog Named Christmas*
and other novels

"In *Talking with Dogs and Cats* Tim Link brilliantly teaches you in a very short time how to engage with and understand your animals organically, giving you the benefits of what took me dozens of years to learn on my own. Once you know the secrets of how to communicate with your best friend, the bond you share together becomes incredibly rewarding and enduring. I highly recommend this book to anyone who has a furry best friend!"

— Mark Winter, cofounder and executive producer,
Pet Life Radio

"Tim Link is a gentle person who has a unique ability that draws animals to him. He has helped thousands of animals through what he does."

— Victoria Stilwell, dog behavior expert and host of
*It's Me or the Dog*

# Talking with Dogs and Cats

# Talking with Dogs and Cats

*Joining the Conversation
to Improve Behavior
and Bond with Your Animals*

## TIM LINK

Foreword by Victoria Stilwell

New World Library
Novato, California

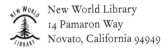

New World Library
14 Pamaron Way
Novato, California 94949

Text design by Tona Pearce Myers

Library of Congress Cataloging-in-Publication Data is available.
Link, Tim, date.
Talking with dogs and cats : joining the conversation to improve behavior and bond with your animals / Tim Link.
    pages   cm
Includes bibliographical references.
ISBN 978-1-60868-322-2 (pbk. : alk. paper)
    1. Pets—Psychology. 2. Pets—Behavior. 3. Human-animal communication.
I. Title.
SF412.5.L56 2015
636.088'7—dc23                                               2015004274

First printing, June 2015
ISBN 978-1-60868-322-2
Printed in the USA on 100% postconsumer-waste recycled paper

New World Library is proud to be a Gold Certified Environmentally Responsible Publisher. Publisher certification awarded by Green Press Initiative. www.greenpressinitiative.org

10   9   8   7   6   5   4   3   2

*To the many animals who have
taught and continue to teach me
almost everything I know about animals;
and to my wife, Kim,
who continues to support me on my life's journey*

# Contents

# Part II: Addressing Animals' Needs and Behavioral Challenges

# Foreword

I've been a dog-behavior expert for many years, studying every available method, technique, and theory, using what works and disregarding what I believe to be ineffective or inhumane. As training ideas have evolved and dogs and cats have become ever more important members of the family, our understanding of what they need to be successful in our domestic environment has also evolved. In the past ten years, the study of canine cognition and behavior, for example, has exploded, with some of the world's finest research universities and organizations making incredible discoveries that will only enhance the lives of our animal friends. This work is not being done by people donning white coats in old-fashioned laboratories, but in normal everyday environments with regular dog owners bringing in their pets to play a series of fun games or negotiate a variety of stimulating challenges. Thanks to science we can now watch how the canine brain responds to certain stimuli in real time and gain even more evidence to validate what we already know: that dogs are smart, emotional, sentient beings that learn much more successfully through motivation and kindness rather than via outdated techniques that punish, inflict pain, or intimidate.

As a science geek, I love what research studies and my own observations have shown, because I'm one of those people who needs proof to support what I believe and teach others. I need to know that my positive, force-free training style is the most effective and humane way to go when teaching dogs and cats, so I can feel comfortable about passing along to my clients what I have learned. I deliver this information with the full knowledge that what I'm doing is backed up with a wealth of well-researched evidence. A whole world of study remains untapped, but that is what makes the field of animal behavior so exciting.

Animal communication exists on a completely different level, but it complements what we as lovers of science and learning are trying to do. I admit that I'm one of those people who thinks the practice of animal communication is a little strange, only because I don't fully understand it. Whatever opinions I might have, though, there is nothing strange about Tim Link. He is an exceptionally normal person. I don't mean this unkindly, I just mean that if you were to meet him, you might be surprised at just how down-to-earth he is, but there is no doubt that Link has an ability that most people, like me, don't fully understand. He's a kind, gentle, knowledgeable person who has spent many years helping people and their pets with all kinds of issues. He just does it in a slightly different way.

*Talking with Dogs and Cats* is packed full of great practical information on how to deal with everyday behavioral issues, along with something less tangible that could take the relationship you have with your cat or dog to a whole new level. In addition, Link offers a wealth of information on how to improve your own life, how not to dwell in the past or the future but to live more in the present, just like our animal friends. We all need to stop for a while and live in the moment, and then — just maybe — we can connect with our animals on an even deeper level.

Even though I'm still pretty useless at it, I am open-minded enough to know that there is more to an animal's "sixth sense" than just a name and that if we take the time, maybe we can tap into something deeper within ourselves to develop a skill we never believed we had — something that will make it easier to understand and talk with our treasured companions. Whatever you believe, I can assure you that positive energy has a positive effect on all our pets, and just being more aware of their sensitivities and emotional needs will greatly increase our understanding and ability to communicate with them.

> — Victoria Stilwell,
> star of Animal Planet's *It's Me or the Dog*,
> author of *Train Your Dog Positively* and *It's Me or the Dog*,
> and CEO of Victoria Stilwell Positively Dog Training

# Introduction

# How You Can
# Join the Conversation

Have you ever noticed that dogs and cats have a particular way of communicating with each other? I'm not referring to the way they greet one another with a thorough smelling of the backside. Nor am I talking about their vocalizations like barking, whining, howling, purring, meowing, and hissing. Though each of these is a particular method in which they communicate with each other, there is more to it than that. What I'm referring to is a different type of communication. Dogs and cats utilize a form of communication that often goes unnoticed by their human companions. They can communicate without any outward noises, gestures, or movements. They know exactly what others want or are thinking without any sound being uttered.

You can watch two dogs lying on the floor beside each other, soaking up the sun beneath a large picture window, sleeping like there is no one else around. Suddenly, they will wake up together, shake their bodies down to the tips of their

tails, stretch, and make their way to the back door to go outside. How did each dog know what the other one wanted to do?
How did they wake up from a deep sleep at the same instant
and go to the door for an outside break? Is it because one dog
knew what he wanted to do and the other just followed along?
Or did they have a quick mental chat about it before they fully
awakened and headed for the door?

As humans, we might wonder, "What is my dog thinking?"
or, "Do my cats like what I do for them?" It's our nature to
want to know what is going on in the minds of our dogs and
cats. More important, we love our dogs and cats and always
look for ways to make them happy and healthy. They provide
us with so much companionship and unconditional love that
we want to make sure we are giving just as much back to them.
We want to do everything we can to make their lives the best
they can be. Have you ever said to yourself, "I wish I could
have a conversation with them like I do with everyone else in
our household"? Well, I'm here to tell you that you can. You
just have to open your heart and mind to the fact that you can.

Each and every dog and cat, as well as all other animals, has
a voice. In this book, I focus on dogs and cats, since they rep-
resent the largest sector of domestic animals. However, over
the years, I've had the opportunity to work with people who
have horses, goats, pigs, chickens, and virtually every other
type of farm animal out there. I've worked with animals that
reside at wildlife sanctuaries, zoos, and aquariums. I've worked
with schools that have rabbits, turtles, fish, and snakes in their
classrooms. If they are furry, feathered, finned, or scaled, I've
likely had a chat with them. Each species of animal communicates in the manner in which they feel the most comfortable,
whether it is through the use of images, colors, words, smells,

tastes, emotions, or any combination thereof. Each animal has feelings. Each animal has a voice and is willing to have a conversation with you if you open yourself up to hear them. So although I focus here on dogs and cats, you can implement a majority of the tools I offer with any animal.

Our dogs and cats not only convey messages to each other but also try to let us know all sorts of things. Sometimes they try to tell us that they need something to make them feel better physically. Sometimes they try to tell us they need something that will bring them joy, like a long walk or playtime outside or with a toy. Other times, they try to tell us they know we are going through a challenge in our lives and they are here to help. Often, they try to better understand what we need from them. Yes, every animal has something to say, and they are just waiting for us to listen — to quiet our minds, open our hearts, and tune in to the words, images, and feelings that they want to share with us.

We are deeply connected with our dogs and cats through a heart connection that is much deeper than we can express in words or verbalize to others. It's something deep within our hearts that goes to the core of our being. We feel this connection but are challenged to adequately describe the depth of those feelings. Our dogs and cats are a vital part of making our lives complete. Our dogs and cats are members of our families and we love them as much as, and sometimes more than, any other member of the family; the relationships we form with them can be as strong as any human relationships in our lives. Our dogs and cats are our constant companions who bring us joy, love, and laughter while asking for little in return. We owe it to them to continue to build upon the deep heart connection that we felt with them the first day we laid eyes on them.

## Slowing Down to Connect with Our Animals

We all have the ability to connect and communicate with our animals at a much deeper level. All we have to do is take the time to better understand *how* to communicate with them on this level. In this all-too-hectic world, we rarely slow down long enough to even know what we are truly feeling, let alone to better understand our animals.

Have you ever awakened, proceeded to go through your daily routine, and by the time you finally took time for yourself, you wondered where the day went? Have you ever caught yourself trying to remember if you completed a task that you planned to complete that day? Can you even remember what you ate for breakfast, lunch, or dinner yesterday? The daily routine can be a good thing, for our animals as well as us. However, routines can become boring at times and offer little in terms of insight for better understanding ourselves, not to mention our animals. Taking the time to slow down to get in touch with your inner self is extremely important for your continued growth and happiness. Slowing down long enough to connect and communicate with your dogs and cats is extremely important for their growth and happiness as well.

We all need to center our energy and keep ourselves in the present moment in order to better connect with our dogs and cats. Our animals live in the present moment; they don't dwell in the past, and they don't wait for the future to arrive. They keep their feelings and thoughts in the present at all times. We need to strive to make each moment as valuable as the next, as they do. Only then will we better understand and be able to communicate with our dogs and cats, as well as every other living creature around us. By focusing our attention and living in the present moment we can get to know our inner selves.

## What to Expect in Communicating
## with Your Animals

This book will teach you to do the following:

- Understand the basic methods of animal communication
- Connect with and understand your animals better
- Quiet your mind and truly listen to your animals
- Trust the information that you receive from your dogs and cats
- Improve your animals' behavior through communicating with your animals
- Understand the emotional and physical effects that change can have on your dogs and cats
- Build a closer bond with your animals

It is important to note that animals have their own free will just like we do. While communicating with them can result in immediate or gradual changes, animals don't always do something just because we ask them to or as quickly as we'd like them to. For example, I had a Pomeranian named Baby. When we adopted her, she was approximately ten years old. She was found by our apartment manager during a severe thunderstorm, cowering in one of the corridors. One of the challenges we noticed immediately with Baby was that she nervously urinated a little bit on the floor in anticipation of being picked up. We later found out from the vet that she also had a hip injury and would yelp when picked up. It took several months of our consistently communicating with her what our intention was prior to picking her up before she stopped yelping and stopped urinating nervously on the floor. So please remember that while communicating with them is essential, it may take time, patience, a lot of love, and, in some cases, changes on our part before we see a positive change.

My intention with this book is to provide you with a straightforward approach that will allow you to communicate more effectively, and at a deeper level, with the dogs and cats in your life. This includes being able to solve everyday challenges that we have all faced at one time or another with our dogs and cats.

Throughout the book, I will offer methods for you to converse with your dogs and cats in ways that I have found to be extremely effective. I will also share a lot of stories about my animals — my past and present dogs (Buzz, Woody, Kramer, Dusty, Baby, Neecie, and Bandit) and cats (Momma Kitty, Natasha, Rusty, and Ash) — and my clients' animals to give you real-life examples. By the end of the book, I hope you will have gained the additional insight necessary to have deeper connections and stronger relationships with the dogs and cats in your life. So, what do you say? Let's start talking!

# PART I

---

## Understanding and Communicating with Your Animals

# 1

## The Animal Connection

Since you're reading this book, I'm assuming you have or have had dogs and/or cats in your life. I'm sure you would say that you have a deep love and bond with each of them. Sometimes it takes a little time for them to work their way completely into our lives. However, for most of us, it was love at first sight and we don't want to think of what life would be without them. Their cute, sweet, and gentle faces always bring a smile to ours. Their soulful eyes connecting with our inner being and expressing pure love is almost too much to handle. Their individual personalities, joyful free spirits, and endless excitement for life are undeniable. It doesn't take long for them to win our admiration and bring about our complete and undeniable attachment to them.

Each dog and cat comes into our life for a specific reason and purpose. It's a much deeper purpose than just providing companionship. Yes, they enrich our lives in numerous ways. But over the past decade I've learned time and time again that there's a much greater purpose at work.

We all would like to believe that we choose the dogs and cats that are part of our lives. Originally, your choice of a dog or cat may have been based on a favorite breed. Or it may have been based on the type of dog or cat you grew up with. Your choice may have been based on the size of dog or cat you're physically able to handle. Maybe you're active and wanted a dog that could enjoy the outdoors with you, or maybe you wanted to provide a stable, happy forever home to a rescue cat or dog. Some people like small dogs, and some prefer large dogs. Some people prefer thick-coated dogs, and others prefer dogs with a short or more hypoallergenic coat. Perhaps you wanted a cat who would lie on your lap, being petted and brushed while you both relaxed on the living room sofa. Some prefer cats who are independent and who don't mind if we live a busy lifestyle outside the home. Whatever the case may be, we all believe we choose the dogs and cats we bring into our lives. However, have you ever had a dog or cat just show up on your doorstep or in your neighborhood and you've been compelled, for some unknown reason, to make the animal part of your family? Have you ever visited a pet-supply store during a dog- or cat-adoption event and unexpectedly taken a dog or cat home? Have you ever searched the internet for a new dog or cat and found that you had an unexplained connection with one of the photos, which resulted in your taking the necessary steps to bring the animal home? We think we choose our dogs and cats, but in many cases they actually choose us, and they invariably bring us unexpected gifts and teach us exactly the lessons we most need to learn at that time in our lives.

I originally chose our two standard schnauzer boys, Buzz and Woody, because the breed is known to be intelligent and easy to train. Schnauzers are also hypoallergenic, which was important because my wife is allergic to most dogs. Also, at twenty-five pounds, standard schnauzers seemed to be just the right size to run with in the park and small enough that we would be able to transport both of them in one vehicle, and, as they got older and their health started to decline, to carry them up and down the stairs without much effort.

I later came to realize that these attributes — the characteristics you can read about in dog books and see with your own eyes — were merely the superficial reasons for our choosing schnauzers. I grew to learn that there was more to it than that — that Buzz and Woody each had a distinct personality, their own purpose to fulfill, and their own lessons to learn when they became part of my life.

Buzz and Woody were more than just canine companions and play partners to me. They both taught me to appreciate the many blessings in life. They both taught me not to waste a single minute in life and to pursue what makes me happy — the things that bring a smile to my face and make me excited about waking up in the morning. Before Buzz and Woody, I had no real spiritual path. I barely took the time to focus on anything outside of work. Until they joined our family, I never would have considered leaving a lucrative corporate career to pursue writing and working with animals on a full-time basis. They each imparted individual gifts to me that I will forever be grateful for.

The cats in my life, Momma Kitty, Natasha, Rusty, and Ash — those that remain of a feral colony of eleven cats that showed up at our house — most definitely chose us. Before that, I'd never had a cat of my own because I've always struggled with cat allergies (though my wife had a Siamese, Little Bit, whom I got to know well when we first started dating in junior high school). I have worked with thousands of people and their cats. I've visited many rescue shelters, including a local humane society where I was president. I've always loved cats and wanted to be around them. But the right and perfect opportunity never presented itself.

Once our cats arrived on our doorstep, that all changed. I got to know all four of them well, especially Momma Kitty. I spend as much time as possible with them, and each has a special place in my heart. Momma Kitty is my constant companion when I'm outside in the garage, driveway, or front yard. She sits beside me and supervises everything that I'm doing outside. Our bond has grown stronger over the years, and I am touched that she has chosen me as her human companion.

Throughout the years, I have seen countless other examples of animals choosing their people and bringing unforeseen gifts to their lives. John was an alcoholic until his dog came into his life. His dog was in desperate need of training and structure, and John could not provide this type of attention while he was drinking. So he gave up alcohol to focus all his attention on training and working with his dog.

Michelle was going through a divorce and had lost all motivation and joy in her life. Her grown children decided to adopt a dog on her behalf to provide her companionship and to take her mind off the challenges she was facing. It worked! Michelle became happy again, and the dog gave her a newfound purpose in life.

Aaron spent all his time working and, as a result, his health was declining and he had stopped socializing with other people. One day, a dog showed up at his doorstep. He felt sorry for the dog and decided to invite him inside. After several days, he decided to take the dog with him to his office. He would take many breaks during the day to walk the dog and get exercise. He met new people and formed new friendships while walking his dog. The dog helped him get physically and mentally healthy again.

I know that our dogs and cats choose us and show up in our lives for a specific purpose. And sometimes their arrival represents what my minister refers to as a "universal two-by-four to the head," making us change unhealthy patterns or learn the exact lessons we need. Once they are a part of our lives, we can recognize and appreciate why they arrived at that specific time.

# 2

## Giving the Animals a Voice

Animals are a vital part of the family, and they can have a significant impact on our lives and who we are as people. Many households have more dogs and cats than people living in them. So why shouldn't the animals have a voice, too?

Animals can communicate and understand one another and often form strong bonds. My two schnauzers Buzz and Woody were inseparable. Buzz was the fun-loving dog who never let much bother him and always went with the flow. He never caused a fuss, and put up with Woody's dominant personality. Woody was extremely loving with his family and the people he knew well. But it sometimes took him a while to accept modifications to his routine and introductions to new people or animals. Buzz never faced these types of challenges. If Woody was unsettled, Buzz would simply sit quietly beside him until he calmed down. Buzz would lean his body against Woody's, as if he were providing a comforting hug.

One time we introduced Woody to a new pet sitter at our

home. He had met pet sitters in the past and knew that it meant we were leaving him with them for the day or while we went away on vacation. On this occasion, he became extremely vocal and wrapped his two front legs around one of my legs as his way of trying to keep me from going. His body trembled and his pointed ears lay back. I had to kneel down, hold him tight, console him, and communicate what was happening. After about ten minutes of my conversing with him, he finally calmed down and understood that we were only going to be gone for the afternoon. My wife and I often spent additional time communicating with Woody to make sure he understood everything that was happening around him. Thankfully, he was intelligent and caught on quickly.

Buzz, on the other hand, greeted the new pet sitter happily, wagged his nubby tail, and allowed her to hug him. This was not Buzz's usual way of greeting people, but he knew that Woody needed to be shown that this person was there to play with and watch over them and that all would be fine. Usually, Buzz didn't show this type of outward emotion and was not vocal with Woody. He would simply sit quietly until Woody felt his calming energy. I am convinced that he communicated with Woody during those times and sent him reassuring messages.

Buzz was usually quiet. He only responded with a slight rumble if we weren't connecting with him when he needed something or when he was displeased. Woody was vocal and often barked, howled, or, if he was really upset, released what sounded like a panicked scream. Often if one dog in a household barks or howls, the others will join in. Thankfully, Buzz knew that Woody was the more vocal of the pair and rarely felt the need to chime in. This balance worked well for them throughout their years together. Buzz allowed Woody to be vocal, while he chose a different, quieter way to get his message across.

Each of our four semi-feral cats has a voice in how they handle matters within their kitty family. They also have a voice with me and aren't hesitant to express their preferences about their care. They purr as they rub against my legs to show me that all is well and they are happy. They meow loudly in disgust when I'm late with their food. They protest loudly when I'm working in the garage, sweeping, or making any other noises that bother them.

Their nonverbal communication comes through clearly, too. For example, when I'm outside in the backyard walking or playing with the dogs, Momma Kitty will sit silently next to the back gate when she needs something. From past experience, I know that this is usually an indication that she needs more food or wants to let me know that the other cats haven't shown up yet. Suddenly, I'll receive a feeling, like a strong message, telling me that Momma Kitty is communicating with me and trying to get my attention. I'll stop what I'm doing and look toward the gate, and, sure enough, she will be sitting there. The dogs don't receive this message from her, only me, since she knows I can hear her and will check with her to see what she needs. Thus, she communicates specifically with me, not with the dogs or any of the other cats in her family.

It is important to stay connected with your animals and aware of what they are doing at all times. If you wait until they sit right in front of you and vocalize or behave in an undesirable way to get your attention, you may miss out on what they are trying to tell you. Don't assume that all is well in your animal's world because they aren't demanding your attention. Often they are trying to communicate with you by simply staring at you or coming near you.

It's important to listen to your animals. Spend quiet time with them, stay connected with their energy, and open your mind and heart to any messages they are trying to share with you. After all, they definitely have preferences when it comes to their wants and needs. They are a vital part of the household and should have a say in everything that happens.

We need to better communicate with our dogs and cats so they better understand what is happening around them. They should be able to share with us what makes them happy and what causes them stress. They should have the same opportunities as anyone else living in the household to know what is happening, what they need to do about it, and why it will ultimately be best for them and everyone living in the home.

Now, I'm not saying they should rule the house, garage, yard, or any other part of the home...though, truth be told, I often feel that my life is centered on my dogs and cats instead of the other way around. Really, that doesn't bother me at all as long as they are happy. We, as human companions to our dogs and cats, are responsible for doing what's best for them. But at the end of the day I still want them to have a say in matters that will affect them. Believe me when I tell you that they often understand matters much better than we do. They usually know what we expect from them and work diligently to follow our instructions. It's up to us to listen to them a little more closely, to communicate better and build the best relationship possible with them. After all, an open line of communication is the best route to achieving a healthy relationship, regardless of whether it's with humans or animals.

It's up to us to continually strive to make their lives the best they can possibly be. Achieving a deep bond and relationship with each of our dogs and cats is essential to living a fulfilling life with them. What better way to build the best relationship possible with our dogs and cats than learning to communicate with them at a much deeper level? We should strive to look beyond the traditionally accepted methods of communicating with them and look for ways to connect more deeply with them.

While structured training, hand signals, and verbal commands are vital tools in helping your animals understand what you need from them, by also using carefully chosen positive keywords, visualization, and positive energy, you can connect with them at a much deeper level. We can communicate what we need from them and see the positive results that come from communicating at this level. At the same time, by opening our minds and hearts and trusting what we receive, we can become better at hearing and understanding what they are trying to tell us. We can share a deeper understanding and relationship with our dogs and cats. We can then provide them with the voice they so deeply deserve.

# 3

## Talking to the Animals

Now, let's dig in and start talking with our dogs and cats! The three simple steps to effectively communicate with your animal companions are:

1. Say what you want out loud.
2. Mentally visualize what that looks like to you.
3. Communicate using a positive tone and positive energy.

Let's look at each of these steps in detail.

### 1. Say What You Want Out Loud

Many people ask what I really mean by "talking" to animals. Surely I don't mean that we have a direct verbal conversation like a human would have with another human, do I? The animals can't possibly understand the words we're saying, can they? They don't hear words like we do, or speak our language, do they?

But the truth is that animals *do* understand us when we

communicate verbally with them. They sense our meaning and moods on other levels as well, but they are perfectly capable of processing verbal information. We should talk to the animals just like we'd talk to any person. They *do* understand what we're saying — and so much more.

## 2. Mentally Visualize What That Looks Like to You

Though we can communicate with animals verbally, as we do with people, one of the most exciting things about interspecies communication (the ability to communicate with any animal) is that we can express ourselves and receive information on other levels. Animals communicate on a more intuitive level than humans do. It doesn't matter if it's a dog in a pack, a cat in a colony, a horse in a herd, or a goose in a flock. They all communicate on a telepathic level: they can connect with other animals' thoughts, wants, needs, and feelings. They know exactly what's going on with each other without ever making a sound.

Human communication, too, is much more complicated than just the verbal information that's exchanged. Interpreting body language is a key to learning how to navigate socially, and subtle auditory elements like tone and inflection make huge differences in meaning. We're so familiar with these elements of human interaction that they've become almost subliminal by adulthood. But with interspecies interaction, it's difficult to navigate with such ease. Dogs' and cats' body language is less intuitive to us, simply because the cues aren't the same. Humans, if nervous, might run a hand through their hair. Dogs, lacking hands, can't mimic this gesture, but they do have body language and other nonverbal cues of their own. If they become anxious, they may pant rapidly, they may put their ears back toward their head, they may pace back and forth or run in a circular movement. As you become more comfortable communicating with your dog, you will pick up on these signals. But in the meantime, you may be tempted to rely heavily on verbal communication to the neglect of more subtle means.

However, the best way to communicate with animals is at a much deeper level. This level resonates at a higher energy vibration and isn't merely reliant on words or sounds. Animals are visual creatures. While spoken language is important, visual images and thoughts play a crucial role as well. For example, when we say a word or phrase out loud, animals hear us with their ears but also visualize what we're saying by forming pictures in their minds.

You may not realize it, but when we speak to animals, we subconsciously (although in this book we'll work to make it conscious) project a visual image that's associated with the words. In turn, our animals see or pick up on this image. They hear what we're saying to them and, more important, they see the picture we're projecting to them. The clearer we are with our spoken words and the corresponding images we project, the more quickly the animal responds.

### 3. Communicate Using a Positive Tone and Positive Energy

Animals understand the meaning behind what we say. When we train animals, we use verbal commands to express what we want, what we need, or how we expect the animals to behave. We use different tones, raising or lowering our voices depending on the command and its urgency. Through repetition of these commands, we believe, the animal will eventually respond. But what about those times when we say, "Stay," for example, and our dog doesn't? We then repeat the "Stay" command and raise our voice or respond with a stronger, less positive tone and energy. We become annoyed, frustrated, or angry that we have to repeat ourselves. The truth of the matter is, a dog doesn't ignore you out of spite or because she is "hard-headed." It's more likely that what the dog saw in her mind in association with your command was unclear, or perhaps she was simply choosing to deflect the negative energy emanating from you. Honestly, can you blame her?

A person's energy or current emotional state affects the communication process. Animals *always* respond better to positive words and positive emotions coming from their human companions. When we use positive words such as "good boy," "great job," or "you're the best cat" in conjunction with positive emotions including excitement, joy, and happiness, we automatically convey our desires at a higher energy vibration. These higher-energy messages are clearer and more pleasant for your cat or dog to receive. They're more pleasant to respond to as well.

It's really simple: positive inflections attract positive results. Your dog or cat wants to make you happy. To that end, she will do everything she can to accomplish what you ask, regardless of whether you're asking her to guard the house while you're gone, quiet down at night, or fetch a stick at the other end of the park.

## Use Precise Words and Images

When we speak to an animal, we need to be precise with the words we use to convey our messages. More important, we

need to be cognizant of the visual imagery that we're projecting as we're speaking. Here are ways that I recommend to do
that:

- Use carefully chosen words to communicate what you
  want.
- Hold an image in your mind that represents what you
  want the animal to hear with those spoken word(s).
- Visualize the expected outcome based on what you're
  saying and the image you're projecting to the animal.

For example, if you want your dog to get into his crate
because you're going to leave the house, visualize the crate and
use the words, "I'm going to run an errand. Please go into your
crate and lie down." The clearer you are with the words and the
associated image you have in your mind, the more quickly, and
more positively, he will respond.

When you use carefully chosen words to share what's on
your mind, the visual images you project will be clear. In turn,
your dog or cat will have a better idea of what you expect from
him and will be better able to respond. For example, if the
desired action is for your dog to go outside to retrieve a stick,
mentally visualize him walking outside, picking up a stick, and
returning it to you. Once you have this series of images in your
mind, open the door, ask him to go outside, get a stick, and
bring it back, while simultaneously picturing what you want
the final outcome to be.

## EXERCISE: The Orange Ball Test

To further illustrate what I'm talking about, let's put what
we've learned into action. Don't worry. This will be easy and
straightforward. This exercise asks you to put yourself in the

shoes of a dog or cat, providing a practical example of how animals hear the words we're saying, how they receive the corresponding mental image behind the words, and how they respond in a positive manner. I call this the Orange Ball Test.

First, keeping in mind what I have said about how animals receive information from us, say the words "orange ball" out loud. As you do so, imagine you're a dog or cat. Then repeat the words a second time. Now answer these three questions:

1.  Did you hear the words "orange ball"?
2.  Did you mentally visualize an orange ball or the letters corresponding to the words "orange ball"?
3.  If you heard the words and saw a corresponding mental image, did answering yes to question 2 make you feel good because you understood the goal of this exercise? If so, you have just lifted your energy to a more positive state, and animals always respond best when we are positive and our energy is at a higher state.

I'm assuming that you heard the words "orange ball" when you said them out loud. After all, the words did come from your mouth. However, the visualization is subjective based on what you projected. When you said "orange ball" you could've visualized an orange basketball or orange beach ball. Maybe you visualized an actual orange. Or maybe you were visualizing the word spelled out — O-R-A-N-G-E.

When you say, "orange ball," to an animal, she may see something entirely different than what you intended. Perhaps she receives the visualization of an orange squeaky ball or an orange play toy that's in the house. A miscommunication may occur if you're preoccupied or in a bad mood, which could lead to your pet being distracted. Out of concern for you, she'd be more focused on your emotional state than on the orange ball. This is why it's important to clearly visualize whichever "orange ball" you want her to receive and do so from a positive emotional state.

Now, I know this exercise may sound silly or seem elementary. But it should provide you with an idea of how animals interpret the words you're saying and emphasize the importance of clear visualization and positive energy. Animals always respond better to positive words, praise, and when we are feeling positive of the outcome of what we need from them.

When my Pomeranian Neecie was alive, she loved to fetch her pink rubber ball. I would throw the ball down the hallway, and she'd run after it and retrieve it, make one trip around the couch, and then bring it back to me. Playing ball with her a few times a day was a real joy and a highlight of the day. She had two balls that were identical in every way except color. They were manufactured by the same company, had the same texture, and smelled exactly the same. One of the balls was pink and the other was orange.

We would throw each ball and tell her to go get the pink ball, and she would bring only the pink ball back to us. We would throw them both again and tell her to get the orange ball and she would bring only the orange ball back to us. Because she played more frequently with the pink ball, we ascertained that she preferred it over her orange ball. So occasionally during our game of fetch she would try to bring back the pink ball instead of the orange ball. However, we would stop her in her tracks, verbalize her bringing the orange ball to us, and send her an image of the color orange or a picture of the orange ball. She would then drop the pink ball and retrieve the orange ball. Later, once you've practiced communicating with your dog using the guidelines in this chapter, you could try a similar exercise with him or her.

# 4

## Trusting What You Receive

One of the biggest obstacles that my clients and students have to overcome when trying to communicate with animals is learning to trust what they receive from the animals they're communicating with. The students follow the steps that I provide, verbalize their communication, visualize the outcome, and usually receive some type of information from their dogs and cats. Some will receive a word or series of words. Others may receive a mental image, a feeling, or an overall knowing that they have successfully connected and communicated with their dogs or cats. Then, out of nowhere, they let doubt creep in and convince themselves that what they received can't possibly be real.

They start to think they just imagined the information they received. They often believe that they wanted to receive information from their dogs and cats so badly that they must have made up the message they received. Well, I'm here to tell you that what you receive is true and you should trust it. Never let self-doubt interfere with what you receive when you are connecting and communicating with your dogs and cats.

Unfortunately, many of us were raised to only believe in something if it can be substantiated with tangible proof. The belief that "if we can't see it and touch it, it can't possibly be real" pervades throughout our society. It is very hard for us to wrap our heads around the fact that something can be real even though we can't touch it or see it with our eyes. We are taught to only accept as fact that which can be proved. Anything outside of that quickly becomes discounted, even if we are the ones who are feeling, seeing, or hearing it.

Most of us are familiar with the sayings "trust your gut feeling" and "follow your instincts." Our intuition, also known as our gut feeling or natural instinct, is the basis of our true knowing. It is a big part of who we are as people and is what we should rely on the most. However, the more we analyze or overanalyze a situation, the more we don't trust that what we feel is real. We start to doubt our instincts even though we know deep down that we should trust them. Trusting and following our intuition is what we all should be doing more of — and it's essential for communicating with our dogs and cats.

When I first started communicating with animals, I instantly started receiving information from them. I would sit quietly in a room with them and begin asking them questions verbally, while visualizing the message I was trying to relate to them. At first, after I asked the questions, I would receive a word or two from them. I would also receive a mental picture of what they were trying to communicate to me. Over time, and a lot of practice, I started receiving a series of words, multiple pictures, and feelings from them. As my ability to communicate with the animals grew, I started receiving smells, tastes, and, if they were ill, the physical sensations they were experiencing.

My gift of communicating with animals opened when I was forty. At that time, all of this was foreign to me and I had my fair share of doubts. At first, I caught myself overanalyzing the information and, unknowingly, letting my own feelings and conscious thoughts influence what I was receiving. I let logic creep in and would sometimes doubt that what I was receiving was real. I remember asking myself, "Is all of this real? Am I just imagining this? Perhaps I'm just guessing and getting lucky when I receive this information. Maybe I should take my luck to Las Vegas or play the lottery because I'm on a roll." As time passed and I practiced more and more, I learned to trust that what I was receiving from the animals was real, and my gift expanded.

When you open yourself to communicate with animals, it is important for you to be in a positive, balanced state. This involves your body, mind, and spirit being aligned and operating in perfect harmony without allowing outside influences to cause disruption. As you communicate verbally and visually, you will receive the information and confirmations you are looking for from your animals. It is now up to you to remove all doubt and trust what you receive.

# 5

# Telepathy Basics

Animals use telepathy as their main method of communi-cating with one another. For example, when a flock of geese needs to change their formation, the lead goose falls to the back of the V to catch the draft and rest. The other geese then move up in the formation, and a new goose takes the lead. Many Canada geese fly over my home during their migration. As they've flown over, I've communicated with them collec-tively and asked them how they know when it's time for an-other goose to take the lead. They've told me that they know this because they communicate with each other telepathically.

Many successful studies involving telepathy have been per-formed since the late 1800s; the first was conducted by the Soci-ety for Psychical Research in London and published in 1886 as the two-volume work *Phantasms of the Living*.[1] The Aborigi-nes of Australia and some Native American cultures have been

---

1   Edmund Gurney, Frederick W. H. Myers, and Frank Podmore, *Phantasms of the Living* (London: Rooms of the Society for Psychical Research, 1886).

known to use telepathy to communicate with other members of their tribes.[2] And certain young children up to the age of five or six years old know how to freely communicate using telepathy — regardless of the distance between them.[3] Unfortunately, because of societal influences, the development of telepathic abilities has not always been encouraged.

"Telepathy" is defined as the acquiring of information from another living being (such as an animal or a person) through the transference of thoughts, ideas, feelings, and mental images. Just as some are born with various natural talents — such as the ability to sing or excel at a particular sport — similarly, all people are born with a natural ability to communicate telepathically. What we choose to do with these abilities and whether we develop them is totally up to each of us.

Animals, on the other hand, use telepathy as their main method of communicating with one another. They don't have to worry about society or peer pressure suggesting that they only communicate in an outward or verbal manner. Whenever you communicate with your animals as described in this book, you're forming a telepathic connection with them that will strengthen your relationship and give you a better understanding of each other.

## Quieting, Centering, and Opening

To successfully use telepathy with animals you must first relax by quieting your mind and body and then becoming centered.

---

2    See, for example, A. P. Elkin, *Aboriginal Men of High Degree: Initiation and Sorcery in the World's Oldest Tradition* (Rochester, VT: Inner Traditions, 1994); and Mary Ann Megegan, *Medicine Men: Power Stories* (CreateSpace Independent Publishing Platform, 2012).

3    See Doreen Virtue, *The Crystal Children: A Guide to the Newest Generation of Psychic and Sensitive Children* (Carlsbad, CA: Hay House, 2003).

Once you've done this, opening a telepathic connection is easy.

To get yourself into the proper state of mind, remember to breathe, relax your body, quiet your mind, and open your heart. This will help you become more centered, focused, and open to receive. Using guided meditations or more traditional forms of meditation are excellent ways to achieve this. If you're unfamiliar with meditation, read a book on the subject or take a meditation class. The health and psychological benefits of meditating have been extensively documented, so you can't go wrong if you establish a practice.

However, it is not necessary to formally meditate. You don't have to light incense, sit on the floor with your legs crossed, and chant to New Age music to meditate correctly. If this works for you and is the way you calm yourself and achieve a state of balance, then by all means continue. But understand that there are many ways to reach the same goal and the method you choose to incorporate into your life should feel right to you. Never let anyone tell you that your way is right or wrong. Meditation should be done as part of your daily routine and in a way that gives you great joy and an overall sense of peace and balance. The form of meditation undertaken or method used to achieve a relaxed state is different for each person.

Being out in nature, taking a long walk, singing, reading, listening to music, and gardening can also put you into a meditative state. There are also many more ways that can take you to that open state of mind. Find that special way of getting to your quiet place where you feel at ease with yourself and everything around you. Basically, perform a task that allows you to become centered and open to your surroundings and circumstances. This space is where you receive inspiring ideas and you feel creative and at your best. When you are in this space, your heart and mind are totally open and you are able to receive intuitive messages, feelings, and the love that is around you. You are at one with yourself and all the joyous possibilities around you. You feel positive about everything and know that everything will turn out well. When you feel positive, your animals will feel positive as well.

I use a combination of methods to quiet my mind, become centered, and allow myself to fully open to receive. One of these methods is to take our dogs to one of the local parks each day. The physical activity associated with walking and running, coupled with the mental stimulation I receive from being out in nature, returns me to my center.

I have also found that being with my cats allows me to unwind. Observing their fascination with the bugs, birds, and flowers around them allows me to feel their calming energy. Watching my cats simply lie in the sun for a long nap draws me into their tranquil space. Simply chatting with them and petting their soft, silky fur makes me forget about all the negative energy and madness that can sometimes creep into my life. Cats are great at teaching us to be one with the world around us and remain in the present.

So, there's no right or wrong method when it comes to relaxing, quieting your mind, centering yourself, and opening your heart to communicate with animals. As long as you find an effective way to get into that space, you will be able to better understand the dogs and cats in your life and connect with them telepathically.

## Tuning In to Your Animals' Frequencies

During my telepathic conversations with many different types of animals, some have chosen to communicate in the form of words, while others have used images, smells, tastes, or feelings.

Animals communicate with a full range of emotions and senses. The method each one uses is based on their preference and how they feel they can best communicate with me.

There are three main forms of telepathic communication. The first form is transmission of feelings, which is the most common form, even among animals. The second form is transmission of feelings and/or images. This is the most common form of telepathic communication between humans. The third form is transmission of words. This form of telepathic communication is the most difficult and requires training.

When my telepathic "door" initially opened (early in 2004 during an animal communication workshop I attended with my wife, Kim), I received most of the information from animals in the form of a word or two. I also received a mental picture in most cases. The mental picture may have been the color of Spot's food bowl, Fluffy's favorite sleeping area, or Rover's favorite toy. As I continued to practice using telepathy, I began to receive a series of words and more detailed visual images from the animals with whom I communicated. As my gift continued to expand, I received feelings and eventually even smells and tastes from them.

In the simplest terms, I like to think of connecting with an animal telepathically as similar to looking for a specific radio transmission. For example, if you knew that your favorite country music station was FM 103.9, you wouldn't tune to AM 750 on your radio to hear it. The fact is that every person and animal has a unique energy frequency, just as each radio station has its unique location on the dial. In essence, once you are tuned in to the right "channel" — your animal's unique energy frequency — you can experience all the wonders of a telepathic connection with him or her.

It can initially be more of a challenge to communicate with

your own animals than with animals who are not a part of your life. Because you are so close to your pets, it is easier to let pre-conceived thoughts and emotions creep into the conversation. You may disregard what you receive because you can see them standing in front of you and you know their personality and the way they behave. It's a lot easier to talk yourself out of what you are receiving from them since you are so close to them. They, too, know your personality and can feel your emotions. They can sometimes talk you out of following through with what you are trying to communicate with them. Think of them as your furry kids. We all know that it's sometimes easier to talk with other people's kids than our own. They know what buttons to push and what they can get away with. Our animals know that if they look at us with soulful eyes and happily wagging tails, we are more likely to give them what they want or forgive them for behaving in a manner that we prefer they wouldn't. It's amazing how a few puppy kisses or kitty licks on the cheek can cause us to forget why we were frustrated with their behavior in the first place.

Often with my own dogs and cats I find that I need to take a breath, center myself, and sit quietly with them to get my full message across to them. They often get so busy playing, running around, or checking out what's going on around them that they don't fully listen to what I'm trying to communicate. In these cases, I simply sit down beside them, pet them softly, and calmly explain to each one what I need to communicate to them, what they need to do about it, and why this will make everyone happy. I also take that opportunity to see what they have to share with me. I have a unique relationship with each of them, and it's important that everyone understands one another and is tuned in to the right and perfect frequency.

My toy schnauzer, Dusty, gets distracted easily. She likes to investigate everything around her. No matter what it is, she becomes fixated and has to check it out. During these times, it is more challenging for me to gain her attention. No matter how many times I ask her to come to me, she will stay focused on the object at hand. I am cautious not to pull her along while she is on her leash, since she weighs only nine pounds and I could injure her if I pulled. Instead, I stop what I'm doing, take a breath, calmly project a message to her that it is time to move on, and visualize us walking away. This usually does the trick: she stops what she is doing and moves along. If she remains fixated, I kneel beside her and speak to her, then send her a series of mental images of all the other places we need to walk to and explore. I tell Dusty that I know she is fascinated by the stick she found (or whatever the distraction might be), but we need to continue our walk to explore new areas. I let her know that I'm pleased she found the stick, but it will make us both happy if we continue our walk.

Momma Kitty seems to understand my telepathic communication clearly. Before leaving the house, I always let her know where I'm going and when I will be back and ask her to continue to lie in her cat bed. When I arrive home, I find her waiting for me in her bed. The only times she deviates from what we had telepathically discussed is when I arrive later than originally planned. In those cases, I find her waiting outside the garage door for my arrival. It's like I'm a kid again and my mom is waiting in the living room for me and asking me to explain why I arrived home past my curfew. Just like with my mom, I have to explain to Momma Kitty why I was late. Fortunately, Momma Kitty hasn't grounded me yet!

It's important to keep the communication channels open

with the animals in your life. Open your telepathic connection with them, trust what you receive, and be open to sending information to them and receiving information from them. This is the most important step you can take to form a deeper relationship with the dogs and cats in your life and all the animals you encounter.

# 6

# Respecting and Understanding Each Unique Animal

Dogs and cats have a deep respect for the humans in their lives. Part of it comes from the fact that we are their caretakers. We ensure they have plenty of good, healthy food and fresh water. We take them to the veterinarian when they're sick. We take them with us for rides around town or to the beach for family vacations. We take them for long walks around the neighborhood or to the mountains to hike the trails. We play with them in our backyards, on our porches, on nature trails, and in parks. We are who they look to for companionship and learn from through our guidance.

Dogs and cats do their best to understand who we are as people and as their companions. They learn from the training we and others provide. They work diligently to understand what we need from them and our expectations of how they should behave. They look for every opportunity to better understand us and make us happy.

In turn, we have a deep respect for the dogs and cats in our lives. We respect them for the wonderful and majestic creatures they are. We respect that all of them have their own unique personalities. Some are strong and outgoing. Others are shy and reserved. We respect their wants and needs and will do almost anything to make each of them happy.

The challenge comes in trying to fully understand them. Getting to know each dog or cat on an individual basis can be a daunting task. We often sit with a puzzled expression, scratch our heads, and wonder, "What in the world is my dog trying to tell me?" or, "Why does my cat keep doing that?" Yes, we respect them, but fully understanding them is another story.

For instance, my beautiful white toy schnauzer, Dusty, loves to pick up and chew on anything she finds on the ground. It doesn't matter if it's a stick, pine bark nugget, or leaf. If it's edible, or she deems that it's at least chewable, away she runs with it in her mouth. I've caught her trying to chew on facial tissue that has fallen on the floor, a piece of lint from a sock, and the cap of a pen. If it's within reach, she will find a way to get to it and start to munch away.

Dusty is young, and I tell myself that she will outgrow this bad habit. After all, puppies will be puppies, right? However, it's my job and responsibility to keep her safe and healthy. So I have gotten into the routine of checking her paws, fur, and mouth to make sure she hasn't confiscated a stray stick or leaf from the backyard before entering the house. It's almost like a security pat down to make sure she is not smuggling any illegal contraband. Once in the house, if she goes off on her own and becomes quiet, I know to go look for her. Nine times out of ten, she has grabbed something she knows she shouldn't have and is chewing on it.

Each time she grabs something she shouldn't, I immediately

ask her to explain her reasons for doing what she's done. She's told me that "it's fun" and that she "likes to chew on things." I tell her that I understand this but that it's unhealthy for her to chew on things she finds outside or we haven't given to her. I ask her to leave these things alone if she encounters them. Then I explain that this will keep her healthy and make me happy because I won't have to constantly worry about whether she has something in her possession that could cause harm. I know that she fully understands this. In fact, we've gotten to the point that she allows me to take the twig or other object away from her without much fuss, and she does her part by supervising me while I dispose of it properly.

By communicating with Dusty, I give her a better understanding of what she should and should not be doing when we are outside. I respect the fact that she is young and loves her outdoor playtime, exercise, and even stick chewing. I have gained a better understanding of her needs while we are outside, too, and respect that she just likes to have fun.

I still haven't gained a full understanding of my cats' need to hunt small animals. I respect that hunting is part of their natural instincts and that no matter how much I communicate with them, their instincts will take over once in a while. But I have communicated to them that I don't want them to harm other animals, no matter what their natural instincts tell them to do. Thankfully, since then they bring me a present in the form of a deceased critter less frequently.

## Unique Personalities

Each and every dog and cat has their own personality. It doesn't matter the breed of the dog or cat, the size of the dog or cat, the household where the dog or cat lives, or the personality of the other dogs or cats in the household. Each has their own style, likes, dislikes, way of carrying themselves, and amount of attention they require. You may have heard that dogs or cats can sometimes look a lot like their owners. But can a dog or cat also take on the personality of their human companion?

Our schnauzer Woody was always the serious dog in our family. He monitored everything going on in and around the house. He made sure his brother, Buzz, was in step with the daily routines and was given plenty of love and attention. If something was amiss in the household, he would let you know, supervise while you corrected it, and give a big "thank you" hug to let you know you did a good job. Woody would often look out the kitchen window to see if anything was going on outside. For example, if he saw the landscapers enter our yard, he would start barking and howling to alert us. Buzz would come running to see what all the racket was for and chime in. This would go on until I went over to the window, acknowledged that I, too, saw the landscapers, and calmly explained they were here to mow the lawn. I thanked Buzz and Woody for letting me know and told them I would be happier if we all went into the living room to play with toys. Once I acknowledged them and let them know that all was well, Woody would stand on his hind legs and give me a hug around my neck, and he and Buzz would stop barking and join me in the living room for some playtime. Woody was a serious boy with a huge heart.

Buzz was the exact opposite of his littermate. "Mr. Happy Go Lucky," he never took anything too seriously and was always up for fun, whether it was a run in the park, a ride around town, receiving his favorite treat, or spending time with the family. If you asked Buzz to do something, he would gladly oblige. He would only get fussy if you took a little too long getting your act together. Buzz was also full of love and pure joy.

I'm sure Woody's and Buzz's personalities were inherent in them. But over the years, I came to realize that their personalities mirrored the personalities of my wife, Kim, and me. Kim also recognized that Woody was a lot like her and that Buzz was a lot like me.

It could be that Kim and I connected with Woody's and Buzz's personalities early on and knew that they were a good match for us. It could be that Woody and Buzz picked up on our personalities, quirks, and nuances and adopted them as their own. I'm not sure what the exact answer is, and perhaps it is a little of both. I do know that they completed our family unit and made everything whole. Woody and Buzz complemented each other just as well as Kim and I complement each other. A perfect balance, yin and yang, with enough love and fun for all!

My cats seem to do as they please and pay little attention to the happenings around them. They notice changes around the outside of the house or around their favorite places to eat and sleep. Though they pop up their heads as I go to the mailbox to get the mail, they can't be bothered to assist. They glance in my general direction when I'm dragging limbs or a pile of brush to our back wooded area to be discarded. But, with the exception of Momma Kitty keeping me company when I'm outside, few things I do seem to hold their interest.

Of course, about the time I think I've got my cats figured out, they'll surprise me. One day I decided that the garage needed to be swept out. It had been a few weeks, or possibly months, since a broom had touched the garage floor. Dust bunnies lurked in each corner, and kitty fur balls rolled across the floor like tumbleweeds crossing the prairie. Each time the mowing crew would visit, they insisted on blowing loose leaves, twigs, and dirt back into my garage through the partially opened door. Needless to say, the garage was a mess! I'm not about to sit here and tell you that I have a high degree of interest in keeping a neat and tidy garage. It's somewhere near the bottom of my list, and believe me, I have quite a list! However, once I'm in the mood to clean, I don't find it to be all that bad.

Momma Kitty's interest while I was cleaning the garage surprised me. Most cats would go running for the hills when they saw the dustpan and broom come off the wall where they hang. But Momma Kitty found it fascinating. Instead of running away, she actually moved closer. She would lie near one of the garage doors while I swept the dirt out into the driveway. She then repositioned herself at the other doorway while I swept that side of the garage. For the final touches, I swept remaining bits of dust into a dustpan and dumped it near the bushes in our yard. With each sweep of the broom, her eyes followed the dust particles, leaves, and fur balls out the door. She was focused on the whole process and supervised every movement I made.

Gardening is one of my least favorite activities. My idea of gardening is sitting with a nice glass of pinot noir and watching Kim plant flowers. The typical scenario when we drive to the nursery is that I sit in the truck listening to the ball game while Kim selects the flowers to put into the planters. Once home, I'll unload the plants, place them by the planters, gather the small shovels, drag the potting soil around, dump the dirt in the pot, and then step aside. Kim knows much more than I do about decorating and placing the flowers in pots to make them look beautiful. If it were left to me, the dirt would go in, a hole would be dug in the middle, and all the plants I could fit would go into the hole. Done!

I've always known that Kim is a master gardener. But I didn't know that one of our semi-feral cats, Ash, was also interested in the hobby. As Kim potted flowers, he would watch her every move. Each time she placed an additional scoop of potting soil in the pot, he watched intently. His eyes would stay glued to her throughout the precise process of tapping down the soil to make sure all the roots were covered and the soil was smooth and filled to the top of the pot. On one occasion, once she finished she turned to Ash and asked him if he wanted to help her pat down the dirt. Without hesitation, he obliged by placing his paw in the dirt at the top of the pot. He then gently patted the top of the dirt several times, putting the finishing touches on the project. The official paw of approval!

I quickly concluded that both Momma Kitty's and Ash's personalities were similar to Kim's. They are thorough and organized with the projects they undertake or supervise, and they all believe in "doing it right the first time."

Learning to respect each of your dogs and cats for the one-of-a-kind animals they are is important for understanding how they act, what their needs are, and who they are. Respect them for who they are, and they will respect you for who you are, even if they don't understand the crazy things that you sometimes do.

# 7

## Past, Present, and Future

We all have a past, present, and future, but how we deal with our past, present, and future is totally up to each of us. Do we handle significant life events, both positive and negative, with grace, or do we get bogged down by them? Do we feel like victims or do we recognize the abundance around us? Do we get so caught up in the past that we can't even begin to see the future, let alone enjoy the present? How we handle our past, present, and future is what matters. Our dogs and cats grasp this much better than we sometimes do.

Our dogs and cats had a past before they entered our life. Some came from other families or had caretakers for a time. Some were born at a breeder or to a family member's dog or cat, then adopted or sold as a puppy or kitten. Some have had wonderful lives and been treated lovingly by their previous human companions. Others have had a rough go of it in their early days, suffering from abuse or neglect. In every case, our dogs and cats have had a past. However, they don't live in the past. Our dogs and cats live in the present. They learn from their past experiences and focus on the present. They don't dwell in the past. They recover from any past traumas, as long as we allow them to.

Unlike animals, most people find it extremely difficult to let go of the past. We spend inordinate amounts of time dwelling on what we could have done better, which leads to feelings of regret. We focus on what material things we didn't have when we were growing up, blaming our parents and society for any hardships we may have faced. Even if our past was wonderful and we were surrounded by a loving family and people in our lives, we sometimes wish the past would have been better. Or we may wish life in the present moment were like "the good old days." We spend so much time and money trying to dissect the past that we forget to live in the present. We also spend much of our lives wondering what our true purpose is and what the future has in store for us. In fact, all the answers are there all along. We simply need to follow the lead of our dogs and cats by living in the present and viewing each day as the wonderful and exciting opportunity it is.

When I'm introduced to a dog or cat who was adopted from an animal-rescue organization or county animal shelter, the human companion or caretaker usually says something like this: "This is one of our rescue dogs named Buddy. He was abandoned by his family, and we want to know about his past and how bad he had it before." Or: "This is my newly adopted cat, Muffin, who I love and am providing a safe and happy home for. I think she was mistreated in the past, and I want to know what happened." In each case, the human companions are focusing on the dog's or cat's *past* instead of how they can make the best life possible for the dog or cat in the *present.* The human companions are surprised when I explain to them that dogs and cats understand their past but live in the present. Once animals know they are safe and have someone to provide for them, they will move on from the past. Each animal is unique and some may take longer to become reassured. But, once they do, they focus only on the present moment and situation. However, as long as we continue to focus on their past, they can't fully let go of it. Our dogs and cats will not fully be comfortable in the present moment if we don't release their past and focus instead on enjoying the present moment.

While you may understandably feel horrible about the less-than-desirable conditions your animal has come from, use the animal's rescue from those conditions as an opportunity to move forward. The past is the past. Nothing can change it. Don't continue to dwell on it. Instead, release the animal's past so that you both can move forward in your lives together.

Most of my dogs and cats have had challenging pasts, but you couldn't tell now. We've made sure to never dwell on the fact that our two standard schnauzers, Buzz and Woody, were within a day of being euthanized at a county animal-control shelter because they were, at ten months of age, deemed too old to sell by their prior owners. Our miniature schnauzer, Kramer, was given back to the original breeder by his prior family because he didn't get along with the wife. All our cats have lived part, if not all, of their time outdoors. They'd sleep and find food, water, and shelter where they could. So, while animals may come from circumstances that we would not subject any animal to, it is essential that we not dwell on those circumstances. Animals don't. Why should we?

My client Darlene adopted a terrier and wanted to know about the dog's past. When I communicated with the dog, he had no desire to discuss his past. Instead, he was more interested in what he wanted to do in the present. He knew that he had an inherent ability to help others heal. His purpose was to assist them in their emotional and physical healing. When I shared this information with Darlene, she was surprised and wanted to know what she could do to assist her new dog. I suggested getting him involved in a therapy-dog program. Her dog would have to pass a series of tests in order to qualify as a therapy dog, but I knew he would be great in this role because he had told me that it was his purpose. I'm happy to report that Darlene's dog is now part of Therapy Dogs International, assisting children in reading programs and visiting hospitals where individuals are physically challenged.

We need to follow our dogs' and cats' lead on this subject. We need to release that negative energy, worry, and concern of the past and focus on enjoying each and every present moment. If we can manage this by creating new memories through positive experiences with our animals, it will make our dogs' and cats' lives happier now and into the future.

# 8

## Animals' Emotions and Sensitivity to Our Energy

Do animals share the same types of emotions that humans have? Do they feel happy and excited when they receive a new toy or are taken to their favorite park for a run? Do they become afraid when a sudden noise startles them or feel anxious not knowing when their favorite human companion is coming home? Do animals feel sorrow or emotional pain when a loved one, human or animal, passes away? The answer to all these questions is: absolutely.

I find that our animals can experience the same types of emotions that we do. They feel the positive energy associated with receiving a treat or going for a hike. They get anxious and fretful when they don't fully understand what is happening with the people and events around them. They grieve, just as we do, when someone they love is no longer around in the physical form. Time and time again I have seen dogs and cats experience the same joys and sorrows that we humans do.

What animals don't allow themselves to do is get caught up

in the ego-driven emotions. Animals don't have the emotions of entitlement, superiority, spitefulness, revenge, and the like. These are all human emotions. Animals don't care what kind of car we drive as long as it gets them to where they enjoy going. If someone wrongs them, they don't dwell on it and look for ways to get revenge. They don't look for ways to show that they are superior to or smarter than the other dogs and cats around them. They don't try to one-up each other and show off in front of other animals. All these ego-driven emotions that we humans experience are foreign to our animals.

How they deal with their emotions is much different from how we deal with ours. Animals are more in tune with themselves and their bodies than we are. They process what is happening around them much more quickly and, if it's a negative experience, look for ways to move past the negativity. By living in the moment, they don't hold on to their negative emotions as long as we humans do. When we experience a negative emotion or event, we tend to hold on to it for way too long. Sometimes, we can't seem to get past negative feelings, and we let them compound until they overwhelm us. If this happens too often or for too long, it can manifest into a physical disease in our bodies. In contrast, if we experience a positive emotion or event, we focus on it for too short a time and let it go too quickly. We should acknowledge those moments and savor them for as long as we can.

## Sensitivity to Energy

Every living thing around us is made up of energy. This is true of trees and plants as well as every person and every animal in the world. Some may call it the universal life force or pure essence of all living things. In humans, we often label this as our soul or our spirit. For our dogs and cats, we can look at it in the same fashion. We all originate from Source energy. We select a body to inhabit when we're born. We live our lives, and then our energy departs the body and returns to the same universal Source (or heavenly space, if you prefer).

While we are all composed of energy, each person's energy is distinct, and the state of our energy can have an impact, negative or positive, on every living being we choose to interact with. We should try to always be cognizant of how our energy affects others.

We have to be especially cognizant of the fact that we have a heart connection with the animals in our lives. They feel the energy we emit regardless of whether it's positive or negative.

They soak up our positive energy like a sponge. They love the energy we exude when all is well in our world. When we are in a good mood and feeling well mentally and physically, our dogs and cats are usually in a good mood and feeling mentally and physically strong as well. When we feel positive about life and surround ourselves with positive people, we find that all is well in our world. If all is well in our world, it usually means that all is well in our dogs' and cats' worlds, too. Staying positive and projecting positive words and feelings to our dogs and cats form a large part of successfully communicating with them, and when we do this, they respond in the positive manner that we expect. Using positive words and feeling good about what you are sharing with them will lead to a happier life and better understanding between you and your dogs and cats.

On the flip side, when we are not in a good mood, our dogs and cats know this as well. They can tell when we are not feeling our best mentally or physically. They can feel the negative energy that we are projecting. This negative energy has a direct impact on them, just as it directly affects us. They don't like how the negative energy feels and often choose to deflect it by not associating with those feelings. That's when we see our dogs and cats leave the room and find a quiet place to be alone. They will often wait until our voice returns to a normal tone and our energy returns to a positive state before they will come back into the room where we are. They may also look for ways to make us happy and return us to a positive emotional state whenever possible.

If we continually expose our dogs and cats to our negative energy or to others' negative energy within the household, after a time they will no longer be able to deflect that negative energy. Instead, they will begin to absorb the negative energy and start to show signs of negativity or illness. Their behavior will change; they will become more anxious, and they may become more aggressive. Sometimes they become destructive with items in the house such as their toys or the furnishings. They can develop physical challenges from holding on to this negative energy.

I had a client named Josie who spent virtually all her time throughout the day and into the night working on her computer. She was a computer programmer and had a small office in the basement of her home. Each day she would feed her cat, Felix, get her coffee, and head down to her desk to begin her workday. After Felix ate his food, he would follow her to the home office and curl up on a small blanket that was placed on a spare chair next to her desk. There they would spend most of the day.

At night, after she and Felix had eaten their evening meal,

she would return to her computer for a couple more hours. She would check her personal email and social media accounts, browse the Web for the latest news stories, or do some online shopping. While she was using the computer during the evening, Felix would return to his blanket on the chair beside the desk and take another catnap.

After they'd followed this routine for years, it started to change. Josie's supervisor asked her to do more work than usual to cover for her coworkers who were less skilled than she, so she began spending even more hours on the computer at night. Often, she would not go back upstairs until late into the night. At this point, Felix stopped spending any time with her in the basement. She thought this was odd but didn't initially do anything about it.

A couple of weeks passed and he continued to stay upstairs instead of following Josie to the basement. A few more weeks passed and it seemed that their routine was beginning to return to normal. One day, Felix followed her downstairs to her office in the morning, and Josie assumed all was well. She sat down in her chair and turned on her computer. Felix, instead of lying on the blanket in the chair beside her desk, jumped on the desk and stood in front of her. He meowed insistently at her while staring her in the face and began to urinate on her keyboard. She of course yelled at him to stop and was furious. He then jumped off the desk and ran upstairs to hide.

After cleaning up the urine, she resumed working. That evening she went upstairs as usual to prepare their evening meals. Felix came out from hiding and rubbed against her legs affectionately. She petted him, they ate, and all seemed fine.

She then went back to her computer as she did every night,

and he followed her. She sat down at her computer and told him *not* to urinate on her keyboard again. He stood there looking at her while she restarted her computer. Within moments he jumped back onto the desk, looked at her, let out a loud meow, and then urinated on the keyboard again. Josie chased him upstairs, and he ran under the bed and stayed there the entire night.

The next day she contacted me and asked me to find out why her cat was urinating on her keyboard. I communicated with Felix and learned that he sensed her agitation about having to spend additional time on her computer instead of being able to enjoy quality time with him. He also said she had been angry while working at her computer during the day and had been typing more loudly than usual. After I shared this information with her, Josie admitted that she had been spending too much time on the computer instead of spending quality time with her cat. Also, she realized that what he had said was true. She had indeed been typing more loudly without being aware she was doing it.

Due to a series of negative changes occurring in Josie's life, including her increased workload, her cat could feel how angry and agitated she had become. He didn't like how her energy felt. So, to bring her attention to the issue at hand, he urinated on her keyboard.

We all agreed it was time for her to breathe, calm down, release the negative energy that she was feeling, spend some fun time with Felix, and walk away from the computer whenever she felt upset. She put the plan into action, and after a couple of weeks her cat was back to his normal routine of enjoying the blanket on his favorite chair.

## Help When We're Feeling Down

Animals can also sense when our physical energy is low or out of balance. When my wife, Kim, or I are not feeling our best on a given day, our animals sense this and try to find ways to help us heal and feel better. When Kim has a stomachache our schnauzer Kramer will curl up close beside her. He will lay his head on her stomach and stay there until she starts to feel better. When I'm feeling a little sluggish, stiff, and sore from recent rains or a bout of cold weather, our schnauzer Dusty gets me up and moving around. She will jump up on the couch where I'm lying, climb on my chest, provide me with a couple of love licks, and then bark and whimper until I'm up and about. She knows I will only feel worse if I lie around all day.

On those rare days when I'm feeling a little disgusted about things, I step outside for a visit with Momma Kitty, who always presents a calm and bright energy. Being in her presence provides me with the calmness I need in order to cleanse my negative energy and return to a balanced state. Even when Momma Kitty is not feeling physically up to par, she never lets it worry her. She instead will rest in her heated cat bed and allow her body to heal. She never complains or causes a fuss. She knows that being upset does not solve anything. She is quite the Zen master!

If you find yourself in a negative state of mind or not feeling well, be proactive and look for ways to return to a state of balance and optimum health. Breathe, spend quiet contemplative time alone, go for a walk, meditate, and do things that make you happy and bring you joy.

You should also communicate regularly with your dogs and cats, following the guidelines I present in this book. Don't be afraid to sit down and have a chat with them. You'll find that you will feel much better after you do. They are wonderful at listening, and you usually get a sweet puppy or kitty kiss afterward to boot!

We can learn a lot from our animals, especially in the emotional department. We need to be cognizant of our emotions and the energy we're projecting at all times when we are around them. If you stay positive, then your positive energy will allow them to have a wonderfully positive life, inspire them to be more open and positive around you, and lead to better communication with them. Staying positive around your dogs and cats will lead to the best relationship possible between you and them.

# 9

# Animals as Barometers

Dogs and cats are in tune with everything that is happening around them. They are sensitive to the changes in energy in their environment and in the people and animals around them. For example, a dog may pace around the house for an hour or more before a storm arrives, or a cat may go into hiding immediately before guests arrive at the doorstep. Is it because their bodies feel differently in those moments, or are they picking up on our emotions and the anxiousness in our energy? Is it their keen sense of hearing that allows them to hear the noises of a storm well before humans can hear them? Or do they feel a change in the barometric pressure? Could it be their overall sense of knowing and their tendency to trust what they are feeling?

Dogs and cats, like humans, have five basic senses — sight, smell, taste, touch, and hearing — that they use all the time. While each of the five senses works in essentially the same fashion in humans, dogs, and cats, some of a dog's or cat's senses are more heightened than those in humans. In a dog or cat without any vision impairment, their sight is much better in the dark compared to a human's. A dog's sense of smell is at least 10,000 times more sensitive than a human's, and a cat's also far exceeds a human's. Also, a dog's or cat's hearing is much better than a human's, and they can pick up much higher frequencies than a human can. Dogs and cats are on par with humans when it comes to the sense of touch, which they use as one method of communicating with one another and with their human counterparts. However, humans win the contest for taste, with around 9,000 taste buds as compared with only 1,700 for a dog and 473 for a cat.

Dogs and cats have an additional, sixth sense that they also use all the time. We humans have it, too, but most of us don't tap into it very often. The sixth sense is the power to discern the true nature of a person or situation, a keen intuition or feeling that is different from the information gleaned from the five physical senses. The sensitivity to energy that an animal feels is a state of being aware and responding to everything in their world. They react to the energy of everything and everyone around them. Our dogs and cats draw from all their senses. They know that using only one or two of their senses doesn't paint the full picture of what is happening. Instead, it represents merely a small fraction of all that's taking place around them.

All living creatures have a sixth sense. I have found that the only differences between a dog's or cat's sixth sense and a human's sixth sense is that they tend to trust what they receive and they use it much more frequently. Dogs and cats are more open to trusting how they feel, never doubting what they feel or where it comes from. Thus, they act upon those feelings accordingly. They sometimes move away from a situation that doesn't feel right. Sometimes they bark or hiss at a person who is giving off a "negative vibe." Basically, they trust what they feel, whereas we sometimes ignore what we feel and the energy around us.

I know for certain that my dog Dusty has a sixth sense when it comes to people with negative energy. It seems that if a person feels "off" to me, Dusty feels it, too, and is inclined to bark at them. Kim and I like to say that Dusty has an internal "bad vibe detector" for people who are projecting negative energy. The nationality, gender, or age of the person really doesn't matter. If they are not giving off positive energy, Dusty detects it within a split second.

On one of our daily drives around town we pulled up next to a car parked in front of a local sandwich shop. We noticed that all the windows were rolled down and two girls, approximately twelve years of age, were sitting in the backseat. Kim and I thought nothing of it, but Dusty immediately began barking and yelping in the direction of the two girls. Kim managed to distract Dusty with a treat as I glanced at the girls. I noticed that each of them had an unhappy look on her face and they didn't seem at all like they wanted to be there. I went into the sandwich shop and noticed a woman in line in front of me. She didn't seem happy to be there and seemed to be rushing the worker who was making the sandwiches. Finally, the woman apologized and stated that her daughters were waiting for her and weren't happy that she had stopped for sandwiches. They instead wanted to get to the pool and skip their lunch.

The next evening we all went out for ice cream. Dusty and Kramer go with us almost everywhere, and they never miss an opportunity for their own small sampling of ice cream. After we pulled into the parking spot, I proceeded to get out of the car to fetch the ice cream for us. Before I could step out of the car, however, a family pulled up next to us and parked their car. In the car were a husband, wife, and two young girls sitting in the back. They were all smiles, laughing and seemingly excited to be there together getting their frozen treats. On this occasion, feeling the positive energy emanating from the family, Dusty began to wag her little nubby tail. She was pleased that the family was having fun and enjoying life. She wagged her tail a little faster when the family recognized her and commented on how beautiful she was.

My recommendation is to always trust your feelings, your own sixth sense. Whenever you're doubting the accuracy of your feelings, pay attention to how your dog or cat is acting. They will definitely let you know if something or someone feels "off."

# 10

# Training and Communication

Training and communicating with your dogs and cats go hand in hand. Communication and visualization are not meant to substitute for positive training. They can, however, be used in conjunction with positive training techniques by providing you with a better understanding of why your dog or cat may be behaving in a certain manner. A combination of proven positive training, communicating verbally, visualizing the results, and emanating positive energy and reinforcement is the best way to help your dog or cat know what the situation is, what you need from them, and why it's a good thing or why they would want to do what you're asking them to do.

I use verbal communication and visualization with my animals every day. For optimum results, I combine these with the excellent training techniques that I have learned from positive trainers. For my dogs, I use hand signals in conjunction with keywords to have them do many things, such as sit before I pick them up, stop barking excessively, lie down for a nap, or proceed with our walk when they've lingered too long in one place. For example, I say, "football," to Kramer when I want him to sit so that I can pick him up and carry him to the truck for our daily ride. I chose "football" as the keyword in this scenario because I hold him the way I would hold and carry a football. This sitting position is different from the one he adopts when I simply ask him to "sit, please" before giving him a treat. I reinforce each hand signal and/or keyword with positive praise and a reward like a pat on the head, a hug, or a healthy treat. If you combine positive training techniques with verbal communication and precise visualization of the expected outcome, you will have even greater success.

For example, when I'm preparing my dogs to go outside for a potty break, I sometimes hear the neighbor's dogs barking. I know that this is going to excite my dogs and will lead to an unpleasant experience unless I'm proactive in changing the anticipated outcome. So, before letting my dogs outside, I stop for a moment to take a deep breath to calm myself. I then verbally explain to my dogs that I know the neighbor's dogs are outside and, as usual, they'll bark and run along the fence, but I need my dogs to remain calm and quiet while outside in order to make the experience enjoyable. While I'm saying these words, I project an image of what I want to happen while we are outside and also visualize it being a positive experience. This allows me to stay calm and feel positive that everything will turn out as I expect. After all, I've already communicated to my dogs what I need from them and why it will be a good thing. Once I've stated this, I feel better for having gotten it off my chest. I remain positive in knowing that all will be well.

Once outside, if they show signs of worrying about the neighbor's dogs in the yard and begin barking and chasing, I reinforce my verbalization and visualization with a training technique and keyword, and this always calms them down. I follow that with praise and attention for doing such a great job. When we have finished our business outside, I ask them to come, and they come back inside with me.

For Dusty, going outside for her potty break is never much of an issue. When entering the screened-in porch at the back of the house before going outside, she barks a couple of times to announce herself to anyone within range. She then runs to the door that leads to her backyard and waits for me to join her. Once in the yard, she spends her time relieving herself and exploring the backyard for new sticks, leaves, or other interesting items that have fallen since the last time she was outside.

She will start barking if a neighbor pulls into their driveway or something startles her. But it's relatively easy to return her focus to the main reason for our being in the yard. When she does bark outside, I take a deep breath and snap my fingers to get her attention. Then I simply thank her verbally for letting me know that someone was there, ask her calmly to continue doing her business, and let her know that we will play and explore more once she has completed her business.

While I'm verbally letting her know what the situation is, what she needs to do, and why she needs to do what I've communicated to her, I project an associated visualization to her. In the case of the neighbors arriving home, I will visualize the neighbors promptly exiting their cars, entering their house, and staying as quiet as possible during the process. This visualization keeps me centered and calm. It also allows Dusty to know that she did her job by letting me know they were home and that everything turned out positively.

As for my miniature schnauzer, Kramer, keeping him from

barking and chasing the neighbor's dogs takes more focus, communication, and visualization. We adopted Dusty when she was a puppy and started communicating with her from an early age. Kramer, on the other hand, was fifteen months old when we adopted him and had never experienced someone using both verbal communication and visualization techniques. He also did not have much exposure to being in a big backyard with neighbors close by. He is a lot more intense and protective of his family, especially when he is outside. Often, he will lose focus on the task at hand and turn his complete attention to the neighbors, neighboring dogs, our cats, or anything that he believes could be a threat. Sometimes, a simple noise will distract him. When his attention is diverted, he will run around and bark loudly. To regain his attention and focus, I take a breath to calm myself and begin patting on the side of my leg until he focuses his attention back on me. Then I reiterate the same verbal and visual information as before. Once I have reinforced my communication with him again, Kramer calms down and focuses on the task at hand.

Since our first attempts to communicate with him verbally and visually, Kramer has dramatically improved. I have been diligent and consistent in my methods of communicating with him over the past eighteen months, and he is getting the hang of it. Kramer has become much more focused and less stressed when he is outside in his backyard. Being outside is much more enjoyable for me as well. When I'm not concerned with how he will behave, he is not as concerned about all the activities going on around him or in our yard. When my energy is off or I haven't communicated with him in advance, he sometimes reverts to his old ways. That's why it is important to stay consistent when communicating verbally and visually with your animals. Combining verbal communication and visualization with proper positive training will always lead to success.

This has worked for Momma Kitty as well. I don't get stressed about what we will encounter when we are outside together because I am there to watch out for her. However, I sometimes let doubt and worry creep in when I am not at the house or am leaving for the day. But she listens intently to me when I explain where I am going and when I will be back and ask her to go into the garage, where she will be safe, dry, and comfortable. On most occasions, when I get back she is in her bed inside the garage waiting for me to return or lying immediately inside the slightly open garage door, peering out to the driveway.

Consistent positive training, verbal communication, and visualization help me to build the best possible relationships and understanding between me and all my animals. It's important to be consistent when communicating with your dogs and cats. Once you have a communication routine in place that works for your animals, communicating with them will become second nature. It's just like riding a bike or flossing your teeth: if you do it enough, you become great at it and it becomes instinctual to you.

# 11

# Keeping Animals Informed

Would you ever leave your house to go shopping and leave your spouse or partner with a list of chores to complete while you were away from home without telling them where you were going and when you'd be back? Would you ever go to work without telling your kids that you were leaving for work and when you'd return home? Then doesn't it stand to reason that you should communicate in the same manner with your dogs and cats? When they see you exiting your house, they, too, want to know where you're going, when you will return, and what they should do in your absence.

We are often in such a hurry to get out of the house to go to work, go shopping, go out for an afternoon of recreation, leave for vacation, or whatever the case may be that remembering to keep those around us — humans and animals alike — informed can be a challenge. We live in a rush, rush, rush world where we feel that we have to get everything completed *now* and we rarely stop to look around us. We often forget to slow down, take a moment to breathe, and have a conversation with the human loved ones in our house, let alone take the time to communicate with our furry loved ones. Some of us may take a brief moment to shout out to our dogs and cats to "be good" while we are rushing out the door. Few ever really inform their dogs and cats about where they're going and when they will return, or provide the animals with a casual, nonstressful job to do while they are gone.

Separation anxiety can have a major impact on our dogs and cats, and I'll discuss that in more detail in chapter 15. For now, suffice it to say that our dogs and cats can become emotionally and physically upset when they aren't informed about what is happening around them. Our animals know we are preparing to leave for vacation when we bring out the suitcases from the closet a week or two before the big trip. When workers come by the house to do repairs, it can upset our animals. And when a guest comes over to visit for the evening, the additional energy in the house and the disruption to the usual routine can affect our animals as well.

Now, I'm not saying you have to sit down beside each of your dogs and cats individually and explain in detail everything that's happening in your world. But if you have the time and it makes you feel better to do so, please do. All I'm suggesting is that you simply take the time before you leave or before an event is about to happen and let them know what to expect. Explain to your dogs and cats what is happening now (or is about to happen) and what they need to do about it. Provide a positive reason why they should do as you ask, or tell them why it will be a good thing for them. If you communicate with them in this manner, they'll handle the situation much better, and you both will be less stressed about it.

I always make it a priority to keep all my animals informed about everything happening in my world, especially if it is going to have a direct impact on them. And when you think about it, everything that is happening in your life — from walking to the post box to retrieve the mail to leaving for a long trip during which you will be away from them for days — does, in some way, affect your animals.

When I am leaving the house to go to the grocery store, I tell my dogs, Dusty and Kramer, where I'm going, that I'll be back in one hour, and that they should take a long nap until I get back. They listen intently to what I have to say and then lie down and go into a deep slumber while I'm away. When I return an hour later, they get up from their dog beds, stretch, and come to the door to greet me. If, on the other hand, I have told them that I will be back in an hour and I'm delayed, they start to wonder why I'm not back home when I said I would be. According to my wife, who is usually there while I'm out, they get up out of their beds after one hour and stand post by the door until I arrive home. They usually bark continuously when I get home to let me know that they are not pleased by my tardiness, until I explain why I was late.

Before we adopted Kramer, we went on a six-day vacation to the beach and took Dusty with us. We left Momma Kitty and the rest of our semi-feral cats at home. We had a pet sitter come over twice every day to visit with and feed the cats. In my rush to get things packed and get on the road for our long drive, I forgot to explain to the cats where we were going, when we would be back, and what they should do while we were gone. According to the pet sitter, for the first five days everything went without a hitch with our cats. They were there waiting for their food each time she arrived. However, on the last day, all the cats took off for a long exploration — maybe in protest of us being gone so long. When we arrived home, none of the cats were there. I'll admit I wasn't too worried about most of them because they like to explore the areas around the house and neighborhood on most days. However, Momma Kitty never left the area around our home. She always stayed in or near our garage where the food, water, and cat beds are located. This time, Momma Kitty was nowhere to be found. Despite my continual communication with her requesting that she return home, she exercised her free will by making the choice to stay away for three days before returning unharmed. It took her a few more days before she would have anything to do with me or show me any attention. She had been upset and confused about why I was gone. She had wondered when or if I would ever return. Despite having her food, water, and beds here at our house, my absence upset her. I was to blame, since I hadn't explained to her in advance what was happening.

Since that one vacation, I have never forgotten to inform the cats, especially Momma Kitty, about what's happening. We have taken several trips since then. I make sure to spend extra time with Momma Kitty before each one to inform her about our plans, what she needs to do while we're away, and that it will be all right. Now she is always there to greet us when we return.

Every time you leave the house, even if you won't be deviating from your standard Monday–Friday routine or are just going out to check the mail, take a few minutes to inform your dogs and cats about where you're going and when you'll be back, what you need them to do or how they are to behave while you're away, and why this will be a good thing for you and them. They will become less stressed about your being away from home and be that much happier when you return.

## Animals' Concept of Time

Have you ever pulled into your driveway and seen your dog at the front door, or your cat sitting in the centrally located picture window, waiting for you to arrive home from work? It's easy to think that they have stationed themselves at that location for most of the day. What dog or cat doesn't like to look outside to see what is happening or to sunbathe on a nice, sunny day? You can even rationalize away their strategic location by assuming they heard your car pull into the drive, heard your car door close, or heard the garage door open. But how do you explain the times when you arrive home from work *early* and your dog or cat is nowhere to be found? There's no dog at the front door and no cat looking out the window. Can dogs and cats tell time? Of course they can!

Now, I'm not suggesting that all our dogs and cats should be wearing puppy and kitty paw watches. (I'm not sure if a company presently manufactures a puppy or kitty watch, but I can see some wheels turning in an entrepreneur's mind as I write this. What a fashion statement that would be, right?) I'm also not trying to tell you that dogs and cats watch the hour and minute hands go around on the wall clocks in our homes. But I know that they know what time of day you come home from work, what time they usually receive their favorite treat, and the difference between your returning in an hour as you said you would and your being forty minutes late.

For the past two years we haven't set an alarm clock in our house. There really is no need to, since Dusty is our personal doggy alarm clock. Since we adopted her, she has always awakened us at 7:35 each morning. It doesn't matter if it is a weekday or a weekend; it doesn't matter if we went to bed at 10:00 PM or midnight the night before. The hours of sleep are irrelevant to Dusty — 7:35 AM is the time to get going in our household, according to her. At 7:35 each morning she awakens in her crate, stretches, yawns, and shakes her body from head to nubby tail. The tags on her collar rattle like an alarm clock, and Kim and I hear her, pry our eyes partially open, squint in the direction of each of our respective nightstand clock radios, and, sure enough, they say 7:35 AM!

Why does Dusty wake us up at that exact time each morning? Perhaps the light is peering in through a window? No, often the room is still dark, thanks to our room-darkening curtains. The only time Dusty's clock is slightly off is when Daylight Savings Time begins or ends. It takes Dusty a few days to adjust, and then her clock is right back on schedule.

Before they passed away, our dogs Buzz and Woody used to have their daily treat routine down to the exact hour and minute they were to receive their treats. At 11:00 AM each day, we had what we called "Kongy time." Each of the dogs had their own red rubber Kong toy, and at 11 o'clock every morning, the dogs would come and place their two front paws on Kim's or my legs. We would be working at our computers and have no idea what time it was. But once the two paws showed up on our legs, we knew it was Kongy time. We would smile, pet each of them on the head, and look up at the clock. Without fail, it would be 11:00 AM.

We would then go downstairs, collect the Kongs, fill them with treats, place them on the dogs' mats, and let them play with their toys and eat the treats as they fell out onto the floor. While they rolled and chased their Kongs around, we would sing a special song that we wrote for this occasion. It was known as the "Kongy time" song.

My client Angie lived with her cat, Angel, for over ten years. Angel never caused a fuss or got into any trouble. Then all of a sudden, her behavior started to change. She became destructive — tearing the curtains off the walls, shredding a comforter that Angie had had for years, and scratching the back of the couch. The destructive behavior had been going on for a couple of weeks, and Angie couldn't figure out what had caused the change or what to do to resolve the problem. So she contacted me, and I had a chat with Angel.

Angel told me there had been a change in the household that she didn't understand. After additional conversation, I learned that the change was that Angie had been coming home from work two hours later than usual for the past two weeks. This change in their routine made Angel uneasy, and the destructive behavior was her way of showing Angie that.

We set a course of action for Angie to better explain her work schedule to Angel. I asked her to tell Angel that she was going to work, how many hours she would be gone, what time of day she would be back, and that Angel should take long naps while she was gone.

Angie implemented the plan and communicated fully to Angel. The next day when she came home, Angel was waiting at the door and nothing had been destroyed. In the years since then, Angie has continued to communicate in this manner whenever she was going to be away from home, and she has never had another issue with Angel.

Our dogs and cats definitely understand the concept of time. So, before you leave the house, always be sure to tell them what time you will be back home. Tell them the number of hours you will be gone. Visualize the hours changing on a clock. If you're going to be gone overnight or for multiple nights, visualize the sun coming up and going down for the number of days you will be gone. Your dogs and cats will understand what you have told them and what you have visualized. They will be less stressed while you are gone, and you will feel better about leaving them at home.

# 12

## Behavior Changes

Dogs and cats usually maintain consistent energy and behavior. Yes, they may get excited and anxious at a moment's notice when they hear a noise outside the house or if they see a jogger running down the sidewalk. However, they are just as quick to move back into the normal, even-keeled energy state that they were in before hearing the noise or seeing the jogger. They don't experience the same level of emotional changes that we do — we can change our emotions and energy level on an hourly basis. It also takes us much longer to release emotions and find that place where our energy and emotions are on a positive, even-keeled state.

I'm not saying that dogs and cats don't feel the same emotions that we do. They absolutely do, as explained in chapter 8. But they seem to process things much more quickly and easily than we do. Our dogs and cats do not have to deal with the challenges of constantly shifting emotions and perceived inability to handle things. However, if their behavior changes and it stays in that state for longer than a day or two, chances are there is a potentially serious issue that you need to address. The issues that cause distress in animals can vary dramatically. But it is up to you to determine what is happening in their world that has caused the sudden behavior change.

If your dog or cat is following the same routine, showing the same behavior as usual, and not displaying any outward signs of trauma or illness, then you may assume that all is well in their world. There's a good chance that you are correct in that assumption, especially since you have a strong bond and heart connection with the animals in your life. However, it's easy to assume all is well when you don't visually see any differences in them. It's easy to get sidetracked with our own challenges in life and forget to slow down to really connect with them. This is especially true with our cats, since they often like their solitude and stay away from us for hours on end during the day.

Fortunately, most of our dogs and cats will let us know if they need something or if something is physically or emotionally wrong with them. Here are some of the direct signs that something is wrong and they are trying to let us know:

- Their appetite changes or they lose interest in their food and treats.
- Their interest in playing with toys or going outside changes.
- They start sleeping for longer periods.
- They become more clingy and needy, demanding more attention from us.

If we notice any of these signs, we have to figure out what the problem is and why our animals are acting the way they are. This is why communicating with our dogs and cats is so important. Slowing down, communicating, and spending time to connect with them on a one-on-one basis is the best way to understand how they are doing physically and emotionally.

My client Susie's cat, Johnny, had always been active and had a healthy appetite, but suddenly one day, seemingly out of the blue, he became lethargic and stopped eating. Susie tried switching the food to see if he would show renewed interest in eating, but no luck. She took Johnny to the vet, and they ran a series of tests but found nothing out of the ordinary. She brought him home and contacted me for a consultation.

After communicating with her cat I uncovered that he always felt sick after eating. To me, it felt like an acidic feeling in the stomach, much like someone with acid reflux would feel. I suggested that Susie contact her veterinarian to see if there was something he recommended to control the associated acid. I also suggested that she have her veterinarian run a complete allergy panel to determine what environmental and food allergies Johnny had.

The test results showed that he had developed food allergies to certain grains and to poultry. After a quick review of the ingredients contained in Johnny's food, Susie discovered that the main protein ingredient was poultry and that the food also contained some grains. She switched his food to one that didn't contain any poultry or grains, and within days he was back to normal.

Dogs and cats can be great at masking their physical challenges. They would prefer to go off on their own to heal a wound or to rest an injury like a hurt leg or hip. They try their best to heal themselves, without causing a fuss or notifying us. It is simply their nature and instinct to find ways to heal without our help. It may also come down to the fact that they know you will take them to the vet if something is wrong physically, and that is often one of their least favorite places to visit. No offense to all the wonderful veterinarians in the world! But do you know of anyone who enjoys going to the doctor?

## Deciphering Changes in Animals' Behavior

Many clients contact me because, out of the blue, their dog or cat has started acting differently. Their dog has become more agitated with the people and other animals in the house. Or their cat has started going off on his own to sleep under a bed or in a closet for hours on end. Or they tell me that their dog quickly eats her food, then wants to go outside and stays there for most of the day. Or their cat stops using the litter box (more on this in chapter 17) or only comes downstairs to the living room after most everyone has gone to bed. In each of these cases, the dog or cat has not shown this behavior in the past.

I will open a line of communication with my client's dog or cat to try to narrow down what is causing the specified behavior change. I like to refer to these sessions as "peeling back the onion." The dogs and cats share with me why their behavior has changed, and then it is up to me to share this information with their family. I then provide suggestions on how to correct the issue.

If, after communicating with the dog or cat, I determine that they are experiencing a physical challenge, I will recommend they visit their veterinarian. Since I'm not a veterinarian, I can't diagnose a physical issue or recommend a course of treatment that involves prescription medication. However, I can provide my client with guidance on what to share with their veterinarian and the physical area that I feel is the issue.

If, on the other hand, it is an emotional issue, I explain to my client what situation is causing the issue. Often it is because of a change in the animal's routine or in the household. I've seen pets be disrupted by all sorts of things: a new baby being brought home without the dog or cat being made aware in advance; holiday visits from family members who are too much for the dog or cat to deal with; family or relationship breakups when someone moves out of the house, causing a lot of confusion in the dog or cat; a child moving away for college or to start life on their own. Anything that can disrupt our lives, energy, or routines can disrupt our dogs' and cats' emotional states, too.

If your dog or cat starts behaving differently, here's what I suggest:

1. COMMUNICATE: Ask your dog or cat what is happening, why they are acting the way they are, and what you can do for them. Trust the first image or feeling you receive and take steps to correct or better the situation.

2. LOOK INSIDE: Often, our dogs and cats will feel the changes going on around them and try to find ways to notify us of what is happening. In these instances, stop what you are doing, take a look at your dogs and cats, take a look around the house, and most important, take a look within yourself. If you do this, you will most likely uncover the cause of the change, either in your dog or cat, in the household, or in yourself. Once you have figured it out, you can work on correcting the issue.

3. BREATHE: Take deep, cleansing breaths in order to clear the energy in you and in the household. Breathing

will allow you to open yourself, stay calm, and be able to focus on the source of your challenges.

It is important to communicate with your dogs and cats throughout the day. Check in with them frequently to see how they are doing physically and emotionally. Keeping everything consistent and providing a calm and energetically positive environment will go a long way toward keeping your dogs and cats physically and emotionally healthy. This will help to curtail any sudden behavior changes with your dogs and cats, too.

# PART II

Addressing Animals' Needs
and Behavioral Challenges

# 13

## Jobs for the Animals

If you've ever taken your dog to formal training or watched any dog-training television shows, you may have heard the saying that to keep a dog happy you need to give them a job to do. You may be wondering if this is also true of cats. The answer is: absolutely yes! Having jobs to do around the house gives cats and dogs a sense of purpose, as well as something to do while you're not there, and stimulates them physically and/or mentally. Some jobs you will assign, and others they will take upon themselves. Either way it's important to understand and respect their roles in doing these jobs.

### Jobs for Dogs

Some people tell their dogs to watch the house while they are gone. Some give their dog the job of fetching an item and bringing it back. Some have their dog carry small items around the house or on walks, in a backpack specifically designed for the dog's weight and size. Others have their dogs follow them around the house to participate in their activities or have the dogs lie nearby when they're not feeling well. Often, dogs take on jobs of their own. They decide what needs to be done at their home and step four paws forward to take on the role. For example, Kramer, my mini schnauzer, has taken on the job of carrying downstairs the toys that our toy schnauzer, Dusty, has picked out. Because Dusty is so small, we always carry her downstairs. Each time we pick her up, she drops the toy she has been playing with. Seeing this, Kramer decided one day that he would make it his job to carry the dropped toy downstairs on her behalf. This is not something we asked him to do or trained him to do. He just decided to do it and has always done it since.

My schnauzer Buzz was always a quiet and laid-back boy. He never caused much of a fuss when he was at home or when we were walking at a local park. He was always amenable to going on long rides and to following our lead in whatever we were doing or wherever we were going. He knew that we wanted him to be a sweet and gentle boy, and he did that job to perfection. However, Buzz had one job that he assigned himself: he was the watchdog when inside the house. Whenever there was a movement or noise outside, he would let us know with a series of barks. The interesting thing was that he never went from window to window or door to door to check out or listen to what was happening outside. Instead, he chose one window of the house as his post: the window in the kitchen near the dinette set. That window is low enough that he could easily walk up to it and sit or stand to check out all things on that side of the house. It overlooks the driveway, the neighbor's house, and the gate leading to our backyard, providing him an optimal vantage point. When he wanted to rest, he chose a position on the couch in the living room where he could lie down and still see out the kitchen window, manning his post from a distance. It was his self-appointed job to patrol things through the kitchen window, and he did his job to perfection.

As I mentioned earlier, Buzz's brother, Woody, was his polar opposite. Though they were brothers from the same litter, their personalities and the jobs they chose for themselves couldn't have been more different. Woody was always on high alert to anything that was happening in the house or outside. Because Woody was by nature extremely sensitive to any changes in the energy of others — humans or animals — if someone entered our house who was nervous or uneasy about being around dogs, Woody would immediately sense this and act accordingly by becoming tenser in his posture and barking at the person for the first few minutes after their arrival. Until the visitor's energy shifted from being nervous and unconfident to more relaxed, Woody would remain unsettled. When Woody was outside in his yard, he was always on high alert to any of the neighborhood dogs playing in their own backyards. He would not tolerate any birds or squirrels entering his yard. The neighbors' repairmen and pool guy were definitely not welcome. He assigned himself as the protector of everything in or around the house. He watched over everything, except the kitchen dinette window — that was his brother's job, and he left that area alone.

Woody assigned himself many other jobs, too. He gave us hugs and love whenever they were needed. He was a great healer, always lying next to me or resting his head on my chest whenever I didn't feel well physically or emotionally. However, the best job that Woody assigned himself was the job of being my muse. Each time I entered my office for a phone consultation with a client, to do a radio show interview, or to write, Woody would be right beside me, lying silently in his bed next to my desk. He would never try to rush me out of the room by barking, wanting to play, or placing his paws on my lap to get my attention (unless he needed something, of course). He would simply lie in a meditative state and provide me with peaceful, loving energy. During those times, Woody was most at peace and filled the room with calmness. He took it upon himself to be my muse, and I couldn't have accomplished the things I did without him.

## Jobs for Cats

Cats, too, need to feel a sense of purpose and have a role, or jobs, to perform to keep their household running smoothly. Many of my clients have said that their cats lie near their computers while they work. Their cats provide them with a sense of calm, especially during hectic times when they're trying to get a project completed. They feel their cat's calming energy, and from time to time glance up to see their peaceful state and reach over to pet or cuddle with them.

Our Momma Kitty is a great example of a cat with multiple jobs. One of the jobs I have assigned her is to let me know when she'd like the towels that line each of the kitty beds to be washed. Admittedly, I don't always have the time to inspect each of the cat beds as thoroughly as I probably should. I also ask her to show the other cats how to do everything at the house in the right way and to make sure every kitty stays in line. She takes these jobs seriously: She lets me know when the towels need to be washed, and she does not tolerate any nonsense, wrestling, or roughhousing among the other cats. She promptly hisses at them and gives them a quick smack on the back of the head if they get out of line.

Momma Kitty has assigned a few jobs to herself, too. She has taken on the role of the official cat greeter and food sampler. My other cats spend most of their days outside playing in the sun and investigating the fields and yards around us. They are all semi-feral and are used to coming and going as they please. They sleep inside the garage at night, eat the breakfast I provide for them, and then off they go for the day. They return at dinnertime for their food and a warm, safe place to sleep. Each morning, Momma Kitty shows them where the food bowls are located (we move them once a week, when the landscapers come) and samples the first morsels. When she has completed her breakfast, she sits patiently while the others finish their meals. She then escorts each of them outside, like a mom taking kids to the school bus stop, and watches each of them leave for the day. When dinnertime rolls around, she walks outside and waits patiently for each one to arrive. One by one she greets them with a quick kitty rub and then shows them to the food bowls. She samples the food, even though she may have already eaten, and sits with them while they eat their dinner. She is quite the hostess.

In several instances, clients have asked me to communicate with their dog or cat because the animal has not accepted a dog and/or cat that they were fostering in their home. In each of these instances, the people hadn't explained why the new animal was being brought into the home or how long they would be staying. I, therefore, communicated with the animals and let them know that this arrangement was only temporary until a permanent home could be found for the foster animal. I then asked the cat or dog who resided at the home permanently to show the foster animal the ropes. This includes showing them where the food and water bowls were, which door to use to go outside to do their business, and where to sleep at night. I asked them to do this job because it would be beneficial to everyone in the house for the animals to get along with one another. In every instance, this approach has proved successful.

## Tips for Assigning Jobs

Here's what I recommend for assigning a job to your dog or cat:

1.  FIND THEIR STRENGTHS: Most cats and dogs exhibit certain strengths or characteristics. Some like to supervise you while you do your work. Some are great healers and cuddle against you when you are not feeling well. Some are great organizers and like to keep everyone and everything in line and focused on the task at hand. You will notice certain traits and skills that your dogs and cats naturally exhibit and seem to enjoy. Assign them jobs related to these skills, and they will be happy.

2.  MAKE IT EASY: Don't assign a stressful job to your dogs or cats like guarding the house, watching the birds and squirrels outside, or keeping an eye out for when the landscapers or postman arrive. These types of jobs will not allow your dogs or cats to relax and can be stressful to them, especially if you are not there to support them. Instead, choose easy jobs like taking a long nap, keeping a favorite blanket warm, or playing with their toys.

3.  BE CONSISTENT: Assign one or two specific jobs to each of your dogs and cats. Don't duplicate the efforts by assigning the same job to any other dog or cat.

When you're assigning a job for the first time, make sure you verbally explain the job, what you need from them, and why the job is important. If the job will be ongoing or repeated, such as your cat taking a long nap every day while you're at work, you don't necessarily need to verbally reassign the job every morning before you leave, but there's no harm in giving them friendly reminders if you want to.

If they have assigned themselves jobs, even ones you don't care for or deem as necessary, try to honor them. I used the example earlier in this chapter about Kramer carrying a toy downstairs on Dusty's behalf. Even though I don't deem this job strictly necessary — there are plenty of toys on each floor for Dusty and Kramer to play with — I can tell it brings him joy to do it and it makes us smile. So, once per week, I simply carry a basketful of toys back upstairs so that he has them available again to take back downstairs when the time comes. If you honor the jobs they do, your dogs and cats will be fulfilled and feel a real sense of purpose.

# 14

# Socialization of Animals

Humans are usually very social with one another. We also love to socialize with dogs and cats, regardless of whether they are our own. This includes pets that are part of someone else's family, those being housed with a temporary foster family, or those at a local animal shelter and in need of a permanent home. If our circumstances don't permit us to have our own dogs or cats, socializing with dogs and cats at a local animal-rescue organization's facility is a wonderful way to spend time with animals. It's also a valuable way to give back to our communities and provide the dogs and cats with some much-needed love and attention.

As for our dogs and cats, socialization can be a very important part of their lives. Socializing them with all ages and types of people, as well as with other dogs and cats, while they are very young can make for a well-rounded dog or cat. Also, try to get them accustomed to seeing wild animals — such as deer, birds, and squirrels — that they may encounter in the neighborhood, the yard, or on outings. While socialization is important for both dogs and cats, the methods used for socializing cats and dogs are slightly different, in part because dogs tend to be taken outside the home more than cats.

## Socializing Your Dogs with Other People

There are a lot of great ways to socialize your dogs with other people. I always recommend starting outside the house first. This takes away any worry they may have about someone new entering their home or yard. First, take them on a long walk or run at a local park to allow them to exhaust any excess energy they may have. This will also allow them to be more at ease in public places where they may encounter other people. Then, fully communicate to them that playtime is over and you would like to introduce them to some new people who also enjoy being around dogs. Locate a quiet section of the park where people may be walking, sitting, or casually lying on a blanket.

Identify people who show an interest in your dog and who show signs of being in a positive energy state (such as smiling, laughing, and possibly playing with their own dogs). You want to make sure that both you and your dog feel comfortable when meeting new people at the park. Ask each person if they would like to meet your dog. They will likely answer yes and then proceed in the direction of your dog. To make sure you and your dog are at ease with the situation, have your dog sit beside you and greet the new people appropriately. Use some keywords that your dog is familiar with or that you have used when they've previously met new people. I like to use words like "be gentle," "be sweet," or "show them you are a good boy [or girl]." Always remember to choose positive words as your keywords. Use the same words consistently for this type of situation. Stay away from keywords like "no," "don't," or "stop." These types of words convey negative energy, and dogs and cats try to deflect negative-energy words. The positive keywords that I've mentioned are those that my dogs have come to associate with how they should behave around other people. During these introductions, I also visualize the entire situation turning out the way I expect it to. Once the visit with the new people is finished, I thank them and let my dogs know it's time to move on. After the visit, I praise my dogs for doing such a good job. Of course a treat is in order as well.

## Socializing Dogs with Other Dogs

Socializing dogs with other dogs is equally important and can lead to some incredible friendships between the dogs. I recommend using a location that is away from either dog's home, somewhere neutral for each of the dogs. A park with plenty of open space is a great option. I do not recommend enclosed dog parks, since most of the dogs are off leash and busy chasing one another, playing, and exploring the park. This often gets a little chaotic, and it's difficult for anyone to stay focused, people and dogs alike. Make sure each of the dogs is on a leash. Ideally, exercise them in another area of the park before their doggy meet and greet.

If possible, arrange to meet a friend at the park who has a dog that is calm and comfortable around other dogs. Make sure the location is quiet with no distractions from other people or dogs. I recommend starting with a short visit and working your way up to longer visits. Initially, a five- or ten-minute meet and greet should do the trick. Keep in mind that the first few meetings are designed to get your dog comfortable with other dogs. Once you have accomplished this, you and your friend can schedule longer playdates for your dogs.

Before the meeting time, and after your dog has been fully exercised, sit quietly with your dog. Communicate with him about what is going to transpire during the meet and greet. Explain what you need from him during the interaction. Most important, explain in a positive manner why this is going to be a good thing for both of you. Make sure to focus and visualize the entire meeting before it actually happens. Breathe, calm yourself and your energy, and visualize a positive outcome. Then proceed to your scheduled location.

Once everyone has arrived at the previously agreed-to location, remember to remain calm and allow yourself to have a sense of knowing that all will be well and everyone will enjoy the meeting. Allow the dogs to greet each other with a few sniffs. Use the same keywords that you used when your dog first met a new person. Again, positive-energy words like "be nice," "be good," or "be gentle" are good choices.

Once the meet and greet is finished, thank not only your friend but also her dog. As they begin to walk away, be sure to let your dog know that he's done a great job and that it's time to go. Praise your dog as if he's done the best thing ever and let him know you're proud of the good work he's done. Of course, a treat is always a good way to thank him, too.

Once your dog has mastered greeting a calm or familiar dog, work your way up to his meeting an unfamiliar, high-energy dog or puppy. The steps and manner of greeting will remain the same. Greeting new dogs while walking in a familiar park can be a wonderful experience for everyone. However, don't ever assume that someone wants to meet your dog or feels comfortable allowing their dog to interact with yours. Always ask the human companion if they are comfortable with allowing the dogs to meet. Try to do this from a distance before the dogs are next to each other. If the person is not comfortable with the meeting, simply walk away or, if you prefer, step aside and allow them to pass before moving on. If they are comfortable with a meet and greet, then proceed in the same manner as when you met your friend and their dog.

## Start Socializing Dogs as Early as Possible

It's imperative to start the socialization process as early as possible in a dog's life. Getting them used to socializing with people and other dogs as puppies is the ideal situation. You can begin communicating and visualizing with them when they are puppies. Interacting with people, being held, and receiving love and playtime as a puppy makes them comfortable around people.

The same is true of introducing them to other dogs and other animals when they are young. They will begin feeling comfortable with animals of different types and learn from them about how to do things. Though they are puppies, look for opportunities to socialize them outside of the home, such as at local training facilities that offer puppy-socialization classes. Also, look for opportunities to socialize them with other puppies and mature dogs their own size. Eventually work your way up to larger dogs that know how to interact with puppies. Keep in mind that some mature dogs can't handle a puppy's high energy and may become agitated with your puppy.

## Socializing Older Dogs

If you have an older dog or one who was not raised by you from a puppy, that's okay. There is still plenty of opportunity for success in socializing your dog. Just be consistent with the socialization methods mentioned above and show patience with your older dog. Staying positive, communicating, visualizing, and following through will lead to success.

My client Laurie enjoys spending time with her five-year-old rottweiler, Jake, who she adopted recently. She takes him to their favorite park for long walks, runs, and games of fetch. They have a great time together, and their time at the park helps him to stay physically active and mentally stimulated. Unfortunately, Jake was not originally socialized properly and never spent time with many people or other dogs at any park. Thus, to eliminate the possibility of a bad experience at the park, she would only go to the park during times when there would likely be no one else around.

One day, Laurie contacted me and said that she wanted to get him more comfortable around other people and dogs. However, the few encounters they'd had with people and dogs at the park didn't turn out well. She became tense in these situations and would hold Jake's leash tightly. She knew that Jake could feel her stress. In turn, people they encountered were unsure about her dog because of his breed and large size. He also barked a lot at the people and dogs he encountered. The dogs he met felt intimidated and would bark at him and pull on their leashes. The meetings left everyone stressed, and she wondered if she should give up.

I communicated with Jake and explained what going to the park and meeting other people and dogs was all about. I asked him to stay calm and remember to be gentle with other people and dogs so that it would be an enjoyable experience for all. I asked Laurie to reiterate this to Jake before each visit to the park and asked that she follow the steps mentioned earlier in this chapter. I reminded her to breathe, relax, and feel confident that the encounters would result in a positive outcome.

Now, after a few months have passed, they are experiencing consistently positive results. They are both much calmer being at the park with other people and dogs. They have made a few regular playdate friends at the park, and they are enjoying their time together more than ever.

## Socializing Cats with People and Animals

Socialization of cats with people is very important and best to begin when they're just a few weeks old. Allowing them to interact with and be handled by friends and family of different ages and energy levels is optimal. That way, they're exposed to children, who usually have a lot of excess energy and are constantly on the move, as well as older people, who are typically less active.

If you have other cats or dogs in your home, socialize those animals with a new cat or kitten that you've brought into your home as soon as possible. Of course, you don't want to just throw them in together and hope for the best. Instead, you want to maintain control over all aspects of the initial interaction, including how much contact they have with one another and for how long.

My client Cheryl needed to provide a safe and successful introduction between her existing cat of eight years, Phoebe, and a cat she was going to watch while her friend was overseas for an extended period. Her friend's cat, Molly, had never been to Cheryl's house and was not used to other cats. Past attempts to introduce Molly to other cats had not gone well. In each case, Molly had attacked the other cat, whether it was at her home or at the friend's house.

While Phoebe had been the only cat in the house for the past couple of years, there had been other cats in their home in the past. Knowing Molly's history, Cheryl was concerned that the cats wouldn't get along. If this were to happen, she would need to keep them separated for the three months that her friend would be gone.

I suggested to her that she start off slowly by introducing Phoebe to Molly in a neutral location like her screened-in back porch. Initially, I recommended that both cats wear harnesses with leashes attached or that they each be put in their own crate, with the two crates facing each other. This would allow them time to investigate each other while still maintaining a measure of safety. She would be there to supervise if the introduction did not go as planned. Once they showed signs of being comfortable with each other, the crate doors could be opened or leashes could be dropped to the floor. If this went as anticipated, they could all go into the house together. This phased approach would help them to become comfortable with each other before allowing both cats free rein of the house.

I reminded Cheryl that she would need to communicate with Phoebe in advance to explain that Molly was a temporary visitor and that she'd need Phoebe to be sweet and show the visiting cat around. I also suggested that she tell Phoebe that having another cat around would be a good thing and that it would make Cheryl happy to know they got along. I explained how, most of all, it was important to visualize the initial meeting going well, all of them living together successfully for a while, and an overall positive outcome.

She followed my instructions, let go of any worry, and felt positive about the situation. The cats handled the situation extremely well and got along. Phoebe enjoyed showing Molly her house and how things were done. The initial worry and fear were removed, and the introduction happened flawlessly. As a matter of fact, now that Cheryl's friend has returned from overseas, she occasionally brings Molly over to Cheryl's for kitty playdates.

# 15

## Separation Anxiety

Over the years I've received numerous phone calls and emails regarding dogs and cats who become overly anxious when their human companion exits the house. It doesn't matter if the person steps outside for a few minutes to water the plants, goes to work for the day, or leaves on an extended business trip. Some dogs and cats find any separation stressful. They can become unsure of themselves and have no idea what to do while we're away.

In these cases, the dogs and cats may be suffering from separation anxiety. Although this can happen with any animal, I see it most often in dogs. Dogs are pack animals and feel most comfortable in a group. In a household, people are viewed as the leaders of the pack, and dogs take their cues from them. But when the leader leaves the house, dogs can become confused about their role and what they should do in the leader's absence — unless we communicate with them beforehand.

Every member of the household has a job to do, including

the dogs and cats. As mentioned earlier, some of the jobs are assigned by the owner and others are self-assigned by the pet. For example, a dog may choose to guard the house because he's seen that there's a need for protection. Another dog in the house may greet the children every day at the bus stop with the mother. These jobs mean something to the dogs and are important for establishing and maintaining their role within the pack. Like us, they feel at peace when everyone in the household is together and all are living in harmony.

When the pack is abruptly separated — say, when the leader steps out unexpectedly — drastic behavior changes can result. The dog or cat, unable to make sense of the change, assumes something is wrong and can react in a way that is meant to get our attention so that their concern can be addressed. In some cases, furniture may be mutilated, the stuffing from the cushions on the couch may be ripped out, or the decorative pillows may be destroyed. A dog or cat may urinate on the carpets, curtains, blankets, or bed. In some households, many pairs of loafers and high heels have been gnawed beyond recognition. I know of one cat who gets the look of sheer terror when the door is locked, the alarm set, and the garage door opened and closed. She runs for the highest point in the house and won't come down until her owner returns safe and sound.

Our schnauzer Kramer is a momma's boy through and through. He becomes fretful if my wife, Kim, steps out of his view. It doesn't matter if she goes out to the front porch to water the plants or to the garage to place recyclable items in the bin. If she forgets to tell him where she is going, he starts to whine and paces around the room until she comes back into view. Though Kim and I are really good about keeping Kramer and the rest of the animals informed, we sometimes forget. We're only human and we both have a lot running through our minds most of the time. We usually catch ourselves quickly and go back to explain matters to Kramer and the others. Once the situation is fully explained to Kramer, he calms down and starts to relax. He often lies near the area where Kim exited, but he stops whining and pacing and becomes more relaxed about her temporary absence.

Now, the typical nature of any dog or cat is not to become destructive and demolish the house. They don't deal in ego-driven emotions like anger and spite. They want to be the best family members possible. They want to make us happy and maintain peace in the home. However, separation anxiety is a real problem for some pets. So what should you do?

It's important to talk to your dogs and cats to keep them informed about everything that's going on in the house. When you're leaving, let them know where you're going and when you'll be back. Most important, let them know what they need to do while you're away — in other words, give them a job, as discussed in chapter 13. I recommend that everyone in the household adopt the following three-step process, which I refer to as the Separation Anxiety Buster.

## The Separation Anxiety Buster

1. Let your dogs and cats know where you're going (e.g., running an errand, going to the mailbox, going to work, going on vacation, etc.).
2. Let your dogs and cats know when you'll be back (e.g., in a few minutes, eight hours, three days, etc.).
3. Let your dogs and cats know what they are to do while you're gone (e.g., take a nap, chew on some bones, be good for the pet sitter, etc.).

You may be thinking, "Does he really want me to tell all my dogs and cats out loud where I'm going, when I'll be back, and what they should do while I'm away?" To this I say, "Absolutely!" It's the same thing that you'd do with the rest of your family members. Would you ever consider just walking out the door without telling your family where you were going and when you'd be back, and perhaps asking them to do something productive while you were away (such as, "do your homework," "unload the dishwasher," or "take out the trash")? Let me break down each of these steps and provide further explanation.

WHERE YOU'RE GOING: Your dog or cat has no idea of what a business trip entails. They may know what to expect with a mailbox run, but only if they've accompanied you on more than one occasion. It's unfair to assume your dog or cat will understand that you have the situation under control when you leave. For all they know, something could be going terribly wrong. This uncertainty explains the negative reactions that may result while you're away. Keeping your dogs and cats informed is the best way to keep them from getting overwhelmed with anxiety when you leave. When you talk with your dogs and cats, it's best to keep it simple and straightforward: "I'm going to go to work now," "I'm going to the mailbox to check the mail," or "I'm going on a business trip for a few days."

WHEN YOU'LL BE BACK: Next, let your dogs and cats know when you'll be back. If you'll be back later the same day, tell them how many hours you will be gone and let them know a specific time that you'll return. As mentioned in chapter 11, I firmly believe that dogs and cats understand the concept of time, both in hours and time of day. For example, you might say, "I'm going to work now and I'll be back at 6:00 PM, which is in eight hours." Or, "I'm going to the mailbox and I'll be back in five minutes." Or, "I'm going on a business trip to Seattle and I'll be back home Thursday, which is in three days."

If you later find that you will be delayed and unable to return at the originally planned time, take a moment to visualize your dogs and cats. Once you have this image, you know you've made a connection with them. Then silently share with them that you'll be home later than expected. For example, if you'll be delayed by one hour, visualize the new return time on a clock. Trust that your pet has "heard" you and that all will be well upon your return.

WHAT THEY ARE TO DO WHILE YOU'RE GONE: The third and final step is to tell your dogs and cats what they should do in your absence. Assert your role as the head of the family and assign them each one specific job. This could be one of the same jobs that you've previously given them or one of the animal's self-appointed jobs. Whatever it is, make it clear, assign only one job at a time, ensure that the job is appropriate for the length of time you'll be gone, and be sure it's something that won't stress them out. Avoid jobs like "Stand guard and protect everyone in the house" or "Look out the window and keep the squirrels out of the yard." That's way too much pressure!

Always remember to use a positive tone and positive words when talking with your cats or dogs. Avoid using negative-energy words like, "no," "don't," and "stop" when you talk with them. If you tell them "*Don't* tinkle on the carpet, they'll try to deflect the negative energy from the word "Don't." Your instructions will come to them as, "Tinkle on the carpet."

Instead, tell them, "Wait until we come home to tinkle, and we'll take a nice long walk and you can tinkle outside." Assign them jobs like "Lie down and take a long nap," "Keep my favorite spot on the couch dry and warm," or "Play nice with the cat."

The key to preventing separation anxiety is to communicate with your animals clearly, consistently, and in a positive way. Everyone in the household has to participate in this effort. Feel confident that what you're saying will be accepted and understood by your pets. Try to *always* communicate in this fashion. This is not a "sometimes" thing. It's an all-the-time thing.

Note that it isn't necessary to visit with each animal in the house, pick them up, hold them in your arms, look into their eyes, and go through these three steps with them. If you can, and you wish to do this, then go ahead. But otherwise, you can simply stand in the middle of the room and address them as a group. They'll understand what you're saying and projecting, even if they're in a different room.

On the other hand, you shouldn't quickly holler this information to them as you're running out the door, either. This doesn't work for the wife and kids, so it probably won't work for your cats or dogs.

# 16

## Changes in Routine

We all have our daily routines. We get up, take a shower, eat breakfast, drink our cup of coffee, go to work, eat lunch, come home from work, eat dinner, spend time with our family, and then go to bed. Most of us follow this type of routine day in and day out, five days per week. The weekend routines, however, are a little more relaxed. So we may sleep a little later, exercise, run errands, go to a movie, or do any number of different activities. For most families I would venture to say that each week has five consecutive days of following virtually the same routine followed by two days of doing things a little differently.

Much like us, our dogs and cats also have their routines. They get up, they go outside or to a litter box to go potty a few times per day, they eat at least twice per day, they take frequent naps throughout the day, they greet you when you come home, they go for a walk, they spend some time with you in the evening, and then they settle in to sleep for the night. As dogs and cats integrate into your household, they begin to realize that there are five consecutive days when they don't get to spend as much time with you during the day, followed by two days when they get to spend more time with you during the day because you're at home more during those days.

But what happens when your day-to-day routine changes? For example, you get a call from your child's school and are told that your child is sick. You then have to drop everything to drive to the school, pick them up and either drive them to the doctor or take them home to rest. What impact does this have on your routine and the way you feel? Do you feel anxious because you don't know what the doctor is going to tell you? Do you feel guilty for taking time away from work? In turn, seeing your reaction, how does your child react, knowing that you aren't acting like you normally do because of this unexpected change in your routine?

As you know, changes from our everyday routine can have a significant impact on how we feel emotionally, and those emotions can affect those around us, including our animals. Because of their sensitivity to their human companions' emotions, reactions, and energy, they know that something has changed. If you come home at an unusual time, it throws off their routine as well.

Don't get me wrong. Dogs and cats love to greet you and other family members when you arrive home, no matter what time of day it is or how long you've been gone. But they do wonder why you're home early if you haven't explained it to them.

## Informing Animals about Changes in Routine

Regardless of whether the change to the daily routine is temporary (e.g., coming home during the day unexpectedly, going on vacation for a week, taking your dog to the groomer, etc.) or permanent (e.g., you've retired so you're at home more, you've decided to work the night shift instead of the day shift, you're moving to a new residence, etc.), there are three things you should always communicate to the animals in your family:

1.  What the change is (the situation, how long it will last, how it will affect them)
2.  What they need to do during the change to their routine
3.  Why the change is going to be a good thing for them

Let's use the "going on vacation" change in routine as an example of putting these three things into practice with your dogs and cats. At least a month before you actually leave for vacation, you should explain your future plans. Because dogs and cats live in the present moment, they view everything as happening "now." So you should be specific that you'll be going on vacation in thirty days.

Regardless of whether they are going with you on vacation, you should let them know how your plans will affect them and for how long. If they are going with you, you'll need to let them know how you will get there, how long it will take to arrive once you leave your house, and what they should expect once they are there. If, on the other hand, they are not going with you, you'll need to explain what the routine will be while you are away.

A few years ago, for example, I took a vacation with my wife, Kim. I explained to both of our schnauzers, Buzz and Woody, that we'd be going on vacation for seven days and that their grandma and grandpa would be here to take care of them. Although my in-laws always took great care of our dogs and other animals for us when we went out of town, it was never quite the same for the animals as when Kim and I were home to take care of them.

Woody's initial reaction to hearing this news was to sit down, look directly up at me, and let out the all-too-familiar schnauzer "whoo-whoo-whoo." This was his way of saying he wasn't at all pleased with the fact that we were leaving and, furthermore, was even more displeased that he wasn't going with us. So I sat down on the couch with him and his brother and filled them in on the entire plan.

I started by telling them that we'd be gone for seven days and that we couldn't take them with us this time because we were going too far away. I told them that grandma and grandpa would take good care of them and that we'd call every night to see how they were doing. I told them that they needed to help their grandma and grandpa take care of the house while we were gone and that they needed to be on their best behavior so that we wouldn't worry. Last, I told them why this was going to be a good thing for them, too: they would get to spend some time with their grandma and grandpa who they didn't get to see often and who would give them a lot of love and attention while we were away.

Upon understanding what the change was, what they needed to do while we were gone, and why it was going to be a good thing for them, too, they both became more at ease. During the trip, when we called each night to check in, my in-laws told us that "the boys" were great and were enjoying being with their grandma and grandpa.

Momma Kitty usually just goes with the flow. It doesn't seem to bother her if we leave the house, as long as I tell her where we are going, when we will be back, and what to do while we're gone. Usually, I ask her to stay safe and take a nap either under the cherry tree by our driveway or, if it's rain-ing, in her warm bed in the garage. I always follow these steps whether we are going on vacation for several days or just going to the store for an hour.

However, if her routine pertaining to when she is fed or where her favorite cat bed is placed is even slightly adjusted without explanation, she shows signs of stress. She purposely sits in areas of the garage or driveway where she knows I will see her. She stares at me for a long time, communicating and sending me a mental picture asking where her food is or where her cat bed has been placed. If I still don't get the hint, she looks in the direction of where her food dish or cat bed is usually located and then glances back at me to make sure her displeasure is known. I quickly get the hint and rectify the situation. Of course, I apologize to her for changing her routine and let her know that I will do better next time.

So the next time you don't think a change in your pet's routine will have an adverse impact on them, think again. Consider how even small disruptions in your daily routine can affect you. Implement this technique and see how much better they handle the change. I bet you'll be pleasantly surprised!

# 17

## Cats and Litter Boxes

Y ou may wonder what cats' number one behavioral problem is. My answer has remained the same for years: they
suddenly stop using the litter box.

Cats are brilliant, intelligent animals. Few other animals
instinctually know what to do with a plastic box that contains
sand or clay. You can place this box anywhere in the house,
and the cat will find it, use it, cover up the mess, and leave as
if nothing has happened. There's really no training involved.
You just put the box down, let your cat know it's there, and
leave it alone.

The brilliance of the cat also shines through when they miss
their mark and go potty outside the litter box. You may ask, "How
is missing the box a sign of being intelligent?" Well, for the most
part, cats are very independent creatures. Most of the time they
prefer to go to an area of the house and be by themselves. They
enjoy the solitude and stillness of those areas of their home. We
have grown to accept, if not expect, this characteristic in the cats
in our lives — often to the point that we don't see our cats for

most of the day. As long as there's some evidence that our cats have been around and their food has been eaten, we assume all is well in their world. In turn, when something isn't going well for our cats, they know they need to get our attention. So what's the best way for them to get our attention? Missing their mark and going outside their litter box.

## Why Do Cats Stop Using the Litter Box?

It's no accident when a cat stops using the litter box. This is not to say that they won't occasionally have a little accident, but if it happens consistently, there's a problem. Your cat is trying to get your attention and get you to "listen" to them. They need you to recognize the problem and make everything better.

I have seen cats stop using the litter box because they have a medical issue. I have seen cats stop using the litter box because a favorite person in the household has moved out or has died. I have seen cats stop using the litter box because someone has changed the type of litter, moved the box to another area of the house, placed plastic underneath the box and along the walls, or even given them a new litter box. Cats may stop using the litter box for numerous reasons. It is great that they are able to gain our attention and alert us to the fact that something is bothering them. It is not so great trying to figure out why and how we can correct the situation.

Based on my years of experience, cats stop using the litter box for three primary reasons (other than it not being cleaned frequently enough, of course):

- A physical issue
- An emotional issue
- A mental issue

PHYSICAL ISSUES: Not feeling well physically can disrupt everything for cats. Their eating habits may change. Their water intake may change. Their willingness to socialize with people and other animals in the house may change. Their demeanor changes, just as ours does when we're under the weather. When our energy is low and we feel lousy, we don't want to be bothered.

Our cats try to heal themselves by going to their favorite spot to rest. They may want to keep their distance from us and not let on that they're not feeling well. Some cats even try to mask their illness, acting as if all is well when we are around. Then they go back to their favorite spot in order to heal. Only when the illness lingers too long or becomes severe will they try to get our attention. At that point, the best way to get our attention is to stop using the litter box.

Illnesses in cats can take days or weeks to develop to the point that we recognize there's a problem. Usually it takes a consistent lack of using the litter box for us to notice. The most common physical ailments in cats are:

- Bladder infections
- Diabetes
- Hormonal changes
- Intestinal problems
- Kidney sludge or stones
- Liver inflammation
- Thyroid disorders
- Urinary tract infections

All these medical issues can be uncomfortable or painful or can have serious long-term effects on your cat. So what should you do? As soon as you notice that your cat isn't using the litter box regularly, and nothing in or around the litter box has been changed, take her to the vet for a checkup. It's always better to err on the side of caution than to let a small medical issue develop into a major problem.

EMOTIONAL ISSUES: Animals can experience the same emotional issues as people. They become saddened when a family member leaves for college or takes a job that requires them to move away. They feel the heartache of a family member's relationship coming to an end. They feel the pain and grief when someone close (a person or another animal) passes away. Because pets share a deep bond with members of their family, they can also react to the emotions of the people in the household. Cats may choose to stop using the litter box to show *their* feelings about the matter at hand. They may not go back to using the litter box until they understand why there has been a change.

In order to solve these emotional issues, you first need to recognize and acknowledge what the issues are. Based on my experience, you usually feel better about something if you take the time to talk about it. But what most people don't realize is that in addition to talking with the people in the house, they also need to talk to the animals. Since we've established that animals understand what we're saying (through the words we use, the tone of our voice, and the visual images we project to them), why wouldn't we talk to our animals as we would to any other member of the family? Spend some time with your cat and explain things to them in the following manner:

1. Explain what the situation is and what you are going to do about it.
2. Explain what they need to do to help you out.
3. Explain why they'd want to do this and why it'll be a good thing.

This process is similar to explaining things to your children. You want to be clear, direct, and as calm as possible. Here's an example: "Sassy, I know you're upset that Jimmy has left for college. I am, too, and I'm going to try to not be sad. Instead, I'm going to focus on how much fun Jimmy will have. What I need you to do is be a strong, beautiful cat and use your litter box. This will make me happy, and I know you always want to make me happy."

By following these steps, you'll have shared your emotions; you'll feel better; your cat, in turn, will better understand what's going on; and things will return to normal.

MENTAL ISSUES: When a change has happened in the household or in the cat's routine that presents a challenge to them, mental issues can result. These issues can stem from the following situations:

- A new animal being brought into the house unannounced
- Another animal challenging the cat for dominance or "alpha" status
- A change occurring in the household routine
- Remodeling or changing the features of the house
- Relocating the litter box to another area of the house, such as a nonprivate area or a location that is too confined (e.g., a closet)
- Purchasing a new litter box that is a different color, size, or shape

As we've discussed, changes of any type in the household can affect how your cat feels and acts. Cats, like all other animals, like to understand their family's dynamics, including how they fit into the mix. They like to know how they need to act within the family, what is expected of them, what jobs they have, and who's in charge.

In order to avoid any mental issues with your cat, follow the same steps listed above for dealing with emotional issues:

1. Explain what the situation is and what you are going to do about it.
2. Explain what they need to do to help you out.
3. Explain why they'd want to do this and why it'll be a good thing.

Now, to be clear, I am not suggesting you call a family meeting (including the animals) and discuss everything in detail before it happens. You don't have to get the cat's approval by having them meow once for "yes" or twice for "no." What I am suggesting is that you spend some quality time with your cat before any upheaval — major or minor, temporary or permanent — occurs. Just as you would with a child, talk with your pets about what changes are about to take place. Visualize that all the changes will be positive and enjoyable. Release any tension or concerns about things that could disrupt the household. Feel good about the final outcome and be confident that all will be fine. This will make you feel better, your cat will better understand what to expect, and all you will have to worry about is regularly changing the litter in the box that your cat *has* been using.

# 18

## Excessive Barking

The most common issue I'm asked to assist with in dogs is excessive barking. If it's not the main reason a client calls me, it's usually somewhere in the mix. Dogs like to bark to notify us about something they are hearing outside when they are in the house. Dogs like to bark to notify us that they see someone or another animal when they are outside. Sometimes, dogs bark just to announce to the world that they are there and that the location where they are standing is their space. Other times, it seems, dogs bark for no apparent reason at all. And don't even get me started about dogs barking when the doorbell rings. Dogs like to bark, and often we wish they wouldn't — or at least that they'd stop after a couple of barks, which is plenty for most of us.

I know a thing or two about excessive barking in dogs. I've been a proud owner of schnauzers for many years. They are a wonderful, incredibly smart breed. However, since they are terriers, they are prone to excessive barking. This is especially true of my toy schnauzer, Dusty. She is a whopping nine pounds of pure energy and excitement. One of her main jobs, which she assigned herself, is to notify us of everything happening around her. She barks to notify us if the neighbors' dogs are outside or if the neighbors have pulled into their driveway. She barks when the trash truck arrives or when a delivery driver is dropping off a package. She barks if someone approaches her while she's on a walk, and she really lets them have it if they don't stop to greet her. She even barks, or more like sings and howls, when a fire or police siren goes off in the neighborhood. She loves to bark, but she stops once we recognize what she's barking at. Once we let her know that we also hear the sirens, thank her for doing a good job, and then show her some attention, she is happy. She takes her job quite seriously, and she is an expert barker.

My schnauzer Kramer is much less of a barker. He only barks excessively when another dog is near him or near his backyard. He's also not the biggest fan of joggers running down the sidewalk or road when we're taking our daily walk. He can't quite figure out what they are running toward and why anyone would want to jog or run for seemingly no reason at all. However, he is quick to stop barking once we let him know all is well and there is no need to bark.

## Tips for Stopping Excessive Barking

I recommend the following steps if your dog barks excessively:

- DISTRACT: Sometimes dogs get locked into what they are barking at. They go into a zone that they need to be snapped out of. In these cases, you need to distract them with a clap of the hands, a snap of the fingers, multiple pats on your leg, or a wave of your hand in front of them. Use any of these distractions to return their focus onto you and get them to listen to what you have to say. If necessary, repeat this step.

- ACKNOWLEDGE: Always make a point of acknowledging what they are barking about. Make a simple reply in the direction of your barking dog; say something like "Yes, I hear the sirens, too!" Make sure you project positive energy to your barking dog and make light of the fact that the sirens don't bother you, and they shouldn't worry about them either. If they are barking while looking out a window or door, you may wish to visit the window or door with them. Take a look outside and say something like "Yes, I see the delivery driver outside in our driveway, too."

- PRAISE: After you've acknowledged why they barked, and they have stopped barking and redirected their focus to what you're saying to them, praise and thank them for doing a good job in letting you know they saw or heard something. Say something like "Great job! Thank you for letting me know there's a squirrel in our yard." If you're near them, give them a gentle pat and praise them again for their efforts.

- REWARD: After you have praised them for doing a good job, reward them. It can be as simple as inviting them for a walk or to lie beside you on the couch while you watch television. Or you can give them a treat or reward them with some playtime.

Depending on the circumstance and your dog's need to bark in association with certain triggers, you can combine the steps above or use them independently of one another. I recommend using whichever step or steps result in your dog barking only a reasonable amount for the situation at hand and then returning to their normal activity.

It may feel odd at first providing praise to your dog when they are barking their heads off. It may feel counterproductive to reward them for something you wish they wouldn't do. However, this is a job that they have assigned themselves. In some breeds and with certain personalities, cautionary barking may feel natural to the dog. But if you follow these steps, your dog will learn that it's acceptable to bark to alert you to something they deem needs your attention, but it's not necessary to bark in excess.

On the other hand, yelling, screaming, or doing anything else that directs negative energy toward the dog will not work. It may provide a short-term fix in a particular situation, but in the long run it will lead them to deflect your negative words and energy and continue with their excessive barking.

Remember to stay calm and breathe when your dog is having a "bark fest." Instead of getting worked up, distract, acknowledge, praise, and reward your dog in order to curtail excessive barking.

# 19

## Riding in the Car

Motion sickness is a fairly common problem with dogs and cats, just as it is with some people. You can reduce or completely eliminate most motion sickness–related symptoms by initially taking dogs and cats on shorter car rides and gradually lengthening the ride time. If you are planning for your dog or cat to travel with you by car in a crate, make sure to get them used to being in the carrier beforehand (also see chapter 21, "Crate-Training"). In some cases, when training and acclimating your dogs and cats ahead of time doesn't work and they still get sick in the car, you may have to give your pet medication to prevent motion sickness, including pet-specific antihistamines, antinausea medication, or sedatives that are prescribed by your veterinarian.

I used to have a beautiful Pomeranian named Neecie. She became my dog during my junior year of college soon after my landlord told me that pets were permitted in the apartment. She loved traveling everywhere with me. I attended a college less than an hour from my parents' house, and I would always take Neecie with me when I went home for a visit.

Though I started taking her for rides in the car as a puppy, she never really liked it. Before we hopped in the car for our ride, I would take her out for a walk because I knew she had a history of getting sick while riding in the car. During the walk she would relieve herself. I would then walk with her to the car and place her in the backseat, and she would lie down. Within a few blocks of my apartment, a foul aroma would permeate from the backseat. I would pull over to the curb, look in the backseat where she was sitting, and see a clump of poop next to her. I knew it had come from her but wasn't sure how she'd had another round of poop in her when she just relieved herself. I felt bad for her and would always try to console her. Fortunately, my college cars were old clunkers with vinyl bench seats that were easy to clean.

Another instance of carsickness that I recall vividly was when Kim and I were taking a young, black mixed-breed dog and a medium-haired black kitten to the local television studio for an appearance on their morning show. The studio was about an hour away from the shelter where the dogs and cats were housed until they were adopted. About forty minutes into our drive we started smelling a foul odor emanating from the back of our SUV, where the dog and cat crates were placed. It was such an overwhelming smell that we were forced to lower the windows.

Once we arrived at the parking lot of the television studio, we parked and immediately opened the back of the SUV where the dog and kitten were in their respective crates. We checked to see who had gotten sick from the car ride. We checked on the dog first, and he seemed to be okay. While he seemed to be feeling fine after the car ride, he was glad to get some fresh air when I opened the SUV door. We then turned our attention to the kitten and found quite a mess. She had defecated all over the back of the crate and the towel she had been lying on. We reached into the crate, picked her up, and attempted to wipe the mess from her backside. However, the mess was wet and had clung to her fur. Also, the smell was too much for us to bear.

Kim put the kitten in a smaller cat carrier and took her inside to the bathroom to wash her. We only had fifteen minutes before appearing on the show and rushed to make the kitten presentable. Meanwhile, I was left to clean the kitty crate and gather the dog for the show. The smell was one of the worst I have ever experienced. It was so putrid that I started to gag and nearly got sick myself. While I was busy trying to clean up the mess and gain my composure, I heard another gagging sound coming from the back of the SUV. This time it wasn't me. Instead, it was coming from the dog. I stopped cleaning and quickly turned in the direction of the dog, but it was too late. The smell was so bad that he had vomited in his crate. I pulled him from his crate, wiped his face with a wet paper towel, and hurried into the studio for our appearance.

Fortunately, we had just enough time to clean the dog and kitten sufficiently to still make our scheduled appearance. The dog and kitten were an overwhelming success, and each showed their sweet personality for all the viewers to see. After the show was finished, we still had an hour's drive back to the rescue shelter. We spent some time with the dog and kitten before placing them in their crates for the journey back. I explained to them what to expect and asked them to let me know if they felt sick during the drive. We praised them for doing such great work and gave them some love. During the ride back to the shelter, not a sound was heard and no overpowering aromas emanated from the back of the SUV. The dog and kitten slept the entire trip back to the shelter. Once we arrived, the shelter manager told us the phones had been ringing off the hook. People had seen the dog and kitten and were interested in adopting them. A couple days later the dog and kitten were adopted, and now they live at their right and perfect homes.

## Acclimating Animals to Riding in the Car

I recommend to my clients that they get their dogs and cats used to riding in the car by staging out the process. Start by telling your dog or cat that you would like to show them the car and ask them to just get comfortable and view the car as a fun and safe place to be. Let them know that it makes you happy that they will be seeing the inside of your car. Then, place your dog or cat inside the car. Make sure they are secured with a leash or harness or are in a crate so they won't escape as soon as you open the door. Sit beside them while they are in the crate or hold them on your lap with their leash or harness on in the passenger seat. Leave the car parked in the driveway or garage — do not start it at this point. Instead, allow your dog or cat some time to get used to being in the car. Allow them to look out the window, smell the smells inside the car, and just get comfortable being there. Allow them to realize that being in the car is not anything to be worried about and that it's actually a good place to be. After they get comfortable, bring them back inside the house. Praise them for doing such great work and give them some attention or a special treat.

Once you notice that they have become comfortable being in the car while it is parked (how long this may take varies considerably, depending on the animal), follow the same process the next time, but this time start the car and leave it parked. As always, make sure the area is well ventilated while the car idles. Allow them to get used to the sound of the engine running. Once they are comfortable with this step, turn off the car, take them back inside the house, and praise them again for doing such a great job.

The next step is to drive the car to the end of the driveway or block and then back again. Once your dog or cat is comfortable with the car moving for a short distance, go a little farther the next time. Drive around the block. If all continues to go well, drive to a pet-supply store or an ice-cream parlor for a special treat. On the next car ride, try driving to a park across town or to a quiet spot for a little picnic or relaxation. Eventually, if you follow these steps, you will be able to successfully extend the car rides farther and farther.

## Tips for Eliminating Motion Sickness

I've learned over the years that motion sickness for dogs and cats is a lot like the motion sickness we experience. Stress definitely contributes to it. Staying calm before, during, and after the trip is important for us as well as our animals. Here are a few other helpful tips that I've used over the years that have worked well:

- GINGER COOKIES, TEA, OR TREATS: Ginger helps to relieve nausea and can prevent motion sickness on shorter trips. Several manufacturers make dog and cat treats containing ginger. Check your local pet store or search online. Or give your animal ginger tea.
- AIR: Rolling down the windows slightly or aiming an air-conditioning vent in their face seems to do the trick.

- No Food: Do not feed your dog or cat a full meal within three hours of a trip (feeding a few ginger treats should be okay). A full stomach that starts to feel uneasy during the trip could trigger messy results.
- Facing Forward or Backward in the Car: Positioning your dog or cat so that they are able to look out a front or rear window instead of looking out through a side window seems to help with stabilizing their equilibrium. It's a lot like when we look toward the side instead of looking directly forward when riding on a roller coaster. Looking toward the side usually makes it harder for us to focus and can lead to feeling dizzy.

## Making Car Rides Pleasant

Make sure that you allow your dogs and cats to ride in the car for positive events. Take them to their favorite places. Make sure they don't associate car rides only with negative locations that they don't like, such as the boarding kennel or veterinarian's office. But when you do have to take your dog or cat somewhere they don't like, make it a positive experience anyway. Go to the boarding kennel and allow the staff to give your dog some attention and treats. But don't leave them there during every visit. Help them realize that sometimes when you go to the boarding kennel it's simply to visit some nice people and then return home. Do the same thing with your cats. Take them to the veterinarian's office just to say hello to the staff and receive some positive attention. Turn the visits from negative experiences for your dogs and cats into positive experiences for all.

# 20

## Storms, Fireworks, and Other Loud Noises

I've never met a dog or cat who didn't get frightened by certain noises and sounds, especially when they happen unexpectedly. I've seen cats who were sleeping peacefully on the front porch become startled by cars that unexpectedly backfired or that had loud music blaring from the windows. The cats become startled, and off they go, running as fast as they can to get away from the sudden noise. These types of noises scare the heck out of me when I'm not expecting them, so it stands to reason that they would also scare our dogs and cats and send them running.

We live in a noise-ridden society and find it challenging to just be in silence. For many of us, even when we are home, it is rare that a television or radio isn't providing background noise and interrupting our dogs' and cats' silence. If it's not our own televisions and radios, then it's coming from our neighbors' homes or their cars when they pull into their driveways.

While some of our animals are startled by even minor noises around the house, others seem to have become desensitized over time to all the noises and choose to not pay much attention to them. They don't seem to get scared and don't even bother to move away from the area that the noise is emanating from. For example, my buff-colored tabby, Natasha, is always cautious of every noise around her, whereas nothing seems to faze my gray tabby, Ash. He will walk across the yard or our fence when the dogs are in the backyard barking loudly in his direction. He doesn't even mind the lawn mower that much. When he hears it being turned on, he casually moves to the wooded area in the back of our house, where he knows it won't bother him.

All sorts of noises can disturb dogs and cats, from common, everyday ones to occasional, special-event sounds. The following are some of the biggest offenders for my dogs and cats, and how my wife and I try to minimize the disruption.

DOORS OPENING AND CLOSING: Things as simple as the raising or lowering of our garage door cause our dogs to bark their silly heads off and cause the cats to scatter like leaves in the wind. The neighbor's car doors and trunks closing startle them all, too. The dogs run to the window, barking to see who may be visiting them. The cats hunker down and hide under a bush or one of the cars in our garage. While I don't have a lot of control over what my neighbors do with their garage doors or their car doors, if I know their routine (when they leave for work, when they leave for school, when they get home for work, etc.), I can communicate with my animals about what to expect and when. At least then these are not completely unexpected events.

LANDSCAPING: The landscapers who take care of our yard and the neighbor's yards generate some of the worst noises of all. The loud lawn mowers, the high pitch of the trimmers, and the rumbling noises from the leaf blowers are almost too much for my dogs and cats to handle. Since our landscapers and the neighbor's landscapers are on a set schedule, I always communicate with my animals and let them know when they're expected to be working in our yard or one of the surrounding yards. Because they know this ahead of time, all but one of my cats will go off and explore in another area of the neighborhood until the landscapers leave. Momma Kitty is the only one of my cats who opts to stay in the garage until they leave. My dogs, Dusty and Kramer, prefer to stay inside with the doors and windows closed until after the landscapers leave. Keeping the windows and doors shut helps to minimize the noise level. And if the television or radio is on during these activities, that helps curtail these unpleasant noises even more.

GARBAGE AND RECYCLING: After returning from grocery or department stores, Kim and I place the plastic bags in a recycling bin. We usually have quite a pile of bags, and we can't help crumpling them as we push them into the bin. This noise always startles our cats, and they never choose to lie anywhere near the recycling bins.

Natasha has a particular sensitivity to the noise the large plastic trash and recycle bins make as I wheel them to the curb and then back into the garage. Before I move them, I have to explain to her what I am doing and tell her to stay where she is and that all will be fine. I slowly move the bins out of the garage, wheel them in the opposite direction of where she is sitting, take the long way around to avoid her, and then gently place them at the end of the driveway. My conversation with her, followed by my cautious movement of the bins, usually does the trick. However, if I forget to communicate with her or move the bins too quickly, she runs from the driveway to a nearby area where the bushes are located, lies down flat on the ground, and watches wide-eyed while I complete my task.

CHILDREN PLAYING: My schnauzer Kramer seems to hate the sound of the neighbors' children screaming as they play outside. Don't get me wrong — my other schnauzer, Dusty, doesn't care for it, either. However, after a few barks and an acknowledgment from us that we realize it's just the neighbors, she will settle down. Kramer, however, will put his two front paws up on the windowsill and stay there barking at the kids until they quiet down or we get him to quiet down using the steps outlined in chapter 18.

YELLING OR LOUD TALKING: Dusty doesn't like it when people talk loudly or yell. This is true even when Kim is upstairs and I am downstairs, and I talk loudly in order for her to hear me. Dusty seems to be overly sensitive to people's energy and doesn't like it when the vocal decibels are raised. She crouches into a ball and tucks her little nubby tail to let us know it bothers her. Fortunately, this doesn't happen too often and we quickly catch ourselves and correct the issue: we have a dedicated attention session with Dusty, communicating with her and assuring her that she did nothing wrong and no one in the house was mad. Of course, we feel guilty afterward because we could have avoided this by keeping our voices in their normal talking tone or by letting Dusty know what was happening before we began hollering.

VACUUMING: We've worked with our dogs regarding the dreaded vacuum and the loud noise it makes. We started by bringing the vacuum out of the closet and leaving it out for several days before using it. This allowed the dogs to sniff and properly check out the big scary beast. They got used to the vacuum being out in the open, and after a few days they started to ignore it, walking by without looking at it and sometimes even lying near it in the hallway. Then we placed the vacuum back in the closet, and the dogs forgot all about it. When we needed to run the vacuum, we would take it out of the closet and let them know we were about to use it. We let them know that we needed them to not worry about the vacuum and told them they would be happy with a clean floor to play and lie on. Now when we turn on the vacuum, the dogs bark a few times and then they're done. They go about their business of playing with their toys until we are done. After we have completed the vacuuming, they walk with us to escort it back into the closet. We thank them for doing such great work and reward them with a treat or some playtime. This method took a short amount of time to implement, some patience, and consistent communication for them to get used to it. Now, hearing the vacuum is a normal part of their routine.

DOORBELL: The front doorbell is a trigger for our dogs, as it is for most dogs. They bark and bark until they're able to see who's at the door. The challenge is that both Kim and I work from home. If the doorbell rings while we're on a conference call, the dogs start barking furiously and it sounds as though a thundering herd is running around the room. We then have to place the call on hold or mute until we can get to the door.

Delivery drivers are the worst offenders, since they always come to the front door. They insist on ringing the front doorbell even though I have a small sign posted that asks them to simply leave packages on the porch and not ring the doorbell. Making matters worse, the delivery drivers are usually long gone by the time we open the door. The dogs don't understand why the doorbell rang and no one was there. This is usually followed by a long series of barks while they search the entire house for the mystery doorbell ringer.

After the delivery driver leaves, I escort the dogs to the front door and ask them to sit. I open the door and tell them that the person has gone. I then close the door, lock it, let them know who was originally at the door, and let them smell the package that was left. I thank them for doing a good job in letting me know that someone rang the doorbell. I provide them with praise and attention before moving on from the doorway. This is all they need to reconfirm what just happened and receive some praise for doing a good job.

Our friends and family know to call our mobile phones when they arrive at our house. We can then meet them in the backyard or in the garage so that the dogs can greet them in a neutral space. This way, the dogs become interested in greeting our friends rather than wondering who may be standing behind their front door. After we greet our friends first, we hand them a couple of treats to give the dogs. They then ask the dogs to sit and wait for their treats. The dogs are more than willing to oblige, knowing they will receive a favorite treat and some attention afterward. Once the initial greeting is complete, I ask the dogs to show our friends inside the house. They take off for the door and wait for everyone to come inside.

FIREWORKS: Fireworks cause anxiety in almost every dog or cat, and many dogs and cats go missing during the Independence Day and New Year's Eve celebrations. Though it's understandable that such loud, booming noises would be upsetting to dogs and cats, I've known people who feel perfectly comfortable bringing their dog with them to watch a fireworks show. Unfortunately, in many cases, when the fireworks launch, the dog takes off. These people quickly seek out my assistance when their dog runs for the hills because the fireworks scared them. As a preventive measure, I don't recommend ever taking your dog to a fireworks exhibition. If you or neighbors set off fireworks in the driveway or yard, keep your dog inside. If the fireworks are so loud that your dog or cat can hear them clearly while inside, I recommend shutting the window blinds and turning on the television or radio to help drown out the noise. I'm all for having fun and enjoying the beauty associated with a city or county fireworks display. But while we may love these events, it's much safer for our pets to stay in the comfort of their own homes than join us in the festivities.

STORMS: A thunderstorm can be one of the most unsettling experiences for a dog or cat. A bright flash of lightning followed by a loud clap of thunder sends many dogs and cats running for cover under a bed or in a closet. While Baby, Woody, and Neecie, three of our prior dogs, reacted by shaking nervously when a thunderstorm began, none of our present dogs or cats have any issues with thunderstorms. We simply communicate with them in advance that there may be a storm and it will be fine. If they are outside when a storm erupts, they quickly retreat inside, out of the bad weather, and take a nap or play until the thunderstorm passes.

## Tips for Calming Animals during Fireworks, Storms, or Other Disruptive Noises

WARN THEM AHEAD OF TIME: Whenever possible, let your animals know that a loud noise is anticipated. If you know that a friend is coming over and will ring the doorbell, or that the Fourth of July fireworks will start at 9 PM, or that a thunderstorm will break while you're at work, tell them in detail what to expect, when to expect it, and how to handle it. As you are communicating with them, remember to use the appropriate visual images to reinforce what you are saying.

STAY CALM: Make sure you stay calm and show no signs of anxiousness about a coming thunderstorm or other loud noise. Your animals will sense your calm state and, in turn, will also remain calm.

PROVIDE BACKGROUND NOISE: When a storm or fireworks show is expected, we usually turn on soft music to provide background noise. Running a floor or table fan can also help to provide white noise in the room.

GIVE THEM A SAFE ZONE: When thunderstorms roll through, clients call me for advice. I tell them to establish a safe zone for their animals. A safe zone can be anywhere that the dog or cat feels comfortable and safe. It doesn't matter if it is in a crate, under a bed, in a closet, under a shed, or anywhere else. If the animal feels safe and secure, then let them ride out the storm in their safe zone.

Whenever a storm was approaching, my Pomeranian Neecie would wake up out of a deep sleep, run to the corner of the room, shake in fear, and often urinate where she sat. This was long before I knew I could telepathically communicate with animals to calm them. Instead, I provided Neecie with a safe zone for her to visit when she was scared of anything around her, especially thunderstorms. Neecie's safe zone was under the master bed. When we saw lightning or heard thunder we would tell Neecie to come with us to her safe zone. She would follow us to the master bedroom, and we would lift up the bed skirt and tell her it was fine. She would crawl under the bed, relax, and not be worried about the thunderstorm any longer.

My childhood dog, a shepherd and collie mix named Bandit, found his safe zone on his own. Bandit spent all his time outside and was easygoing and unafraid. Thunderstorms were the only thing that bothered him. We could always tell that a storm was coming just by watching Bandit. Well before the lightning and thunder arrived, Bandit would head to his safe zone. He had dug out a spot in the ground that led under our outdoor shed. Bandit would crawl under the shed and stay there until the storm passed. He would then crawl out, usually wetter and muddier than if he had stayed out in the storm. He chose being under the shed instead of in his doghouse where it was safe and dry. (Of course, as I became an adult and had more dogs, I never relegated any of them to the backyard to live out their life. Unfortunately, when I was growing up, this wasn't considered an unusual practice.)

When setting up the safe zone, place the crate or sleeping quarters in a place that the animal is comfortable with and likes to visit. Place a padded cushion inside for comfort and a favorite blanket or throw for warmth. You may choose to place a favorite toy inside as well. Spend time near the safe zone and physically show your dog or cat how nice and special the location is. Let them know that you organized it just the way they like it and it is just for them. Allow them to investigate in and around the area. You want the safe zone to be a place where they can visit to feel protected and to relax.

By communicating with your dogs and cats, accompanied with projecting your own calm energy, you can overcome any challenges that storms and loud noises may cause.

# 21

## Crate-Training

When we adopted our schnauzers Buzz and Woody, they were already trained in all the basics. They knew how to sit, lie down, stay, and come. They were fully potty trained and learned quickly which door in the house was their exit point to the great outdoors. They were even crate-trained and actually enjoyed their crates. This was the first experience I had with using dog crates and leaving the dogs inside a crate when I left the house for a few hours.

I have to say, the crates were a big hit in our family. No longer did we need to worry if the dogs would get into mischief while we were gone. If we were a little late getting home, we didn't have to worry about them having an accident on the floor; like most dogs, they wouldn't go potty in the place where they slept. We didn't have to worry about a door frame being scratched or the baseboard molding being chewed to shreds because an unexpected thunderstorm had erupted during our absence. Our dogs felt very comfortable and secure in their crates and never got into any trouble when left there. They each had their own crate — with plenty of room to stretch out inside, on the comfortable mat we provided for them — and we positioned the two crates side by side.

When leaving the house we would simply ask them to go lie down. This would be their notification that we needed them to go into their crates and lie down. They knew we were leaving the house and never seemed to mind as long as we followed this routine. They would enter their crates and wait for a special treat that they received for doing a good job. We would then pet each dog and tell them where we were going, when we would be back, and what they should do while we were gone. The job we assigned them was simple: take a long nap. We made sure they knew how many hours we were going to be gone and sent a visual picture of a clock with the hours changing to match the number of hours we would be gone (as described in chapter 11). This kept their minds at ease, and they slept until we returned home. We never left them in their crates longer than four hours at a time during the day. If we knew we would be gone longer, we had a pet sitter come over and let them out for a walk and to relieve themselves.

Since we have a multilevel home, we decided to purchase a separate set of identical crates for the upstairs level where we all slept at night and for the in-law suite on the main floor of the house. Having a separate set of crates helped us as well as Buzz and Woody as they got older. No longer could they run up and down the stairs to rest in their master bedroom crates. Now, during the day they rested in the crates located in the in-law suite. At night, we carried them upstairs to their crates in the master bedroom. Each night at bedtime, we followed the same routine as if we were leaving the house. We asked them to go lie down, provided them with a special treat, gave them some love, told them when we anticipated waking up, and visualized a clock with the hours changing to match the hours we would be asleep. They would sleep through the night without a peep, awakening us only if we overslept or they didn't feel well. By following this routine, we never had to use an alarm clock again.

When traveling with the dogs, we followed the same routine. We would load the dog crates into the back of our SUV and then lift Buzz and Woody and put them into their respective crates. We would ask them to lie down and provide them with their special treat. We would pet them on the head and explain where we were going and how long we would be en route and provide them with a job to do while we were traveling. The explanation went something like this: "We're going to take a drive to grandma's house and will be staying for three days. It will take us five hours to get there, and we will stop once at your favorite park, which is halfway to her house. I need you to lie down and take a long nap until we make our stop at the park and then again until we arrive at grandma's house." We also made sure to use the visual clock to show the hours changing to match the hours for the stop at the park and our final destination at grandma's house. This worked like a charm, and Buzz and Woody would sleep the entire trip.

## Making the Crate a Comfortable Place

Many types of crates can be used for home and travel. Some are made of metal wiring or canvas and can collapse for easy storage, making it easy to relocate the crate to different locations in the house or away from home or to set it up in the car.

Some are made of a sturdy plastic, so they're easy to transport and easy to clean, if necessary. I suggest trying different crates to see which type your dog is comfortable with and to find one that matches your home and travel needs.

We always place a thick memory-foam pad specifically designed for dogs in the bottom of the crate. We ensure that it is the same size as the floor of the crate. We also place a beach towel on top of the pad and roll up another one for the animal to rest their head on. This provides them extra comfort and support while resting for long periods of time, and we can easily clean or replace the towels every few days. Finally, we place a favorite plush dog toy inside for added security. I suggest skipping the toy if you have a young pup or a dog that likes to destroy toys. You don't want to take a chance of your dog destroying and consuming the toy in your absence.

For dogs who aren't used to crates or have had issues with being in a crate, I suggest the following additional items for the crate:

- COVERING: Place a large towel over the outside of the crate. Leave the front and back of the crate open so proper airflow can circulate. This will provide an extra-secure environment for the dog. It provides a den-type feeling that they will enjoy.

- FLOOR OR TABLE FAN: Place a floor or table fan near the crate and point it in the direction of the crate, or set it to oscillate, on the low setting. The fan will help keep your dog cool and provide white noise that will drown out any noises coming from outside the house.

- RADIO: Turn on a radio or stereo to provide background music for your dog. Find out what music your dog prefers by playing several types of music stations throughout the week. You will be able to tell from your dog's reaction which type of music they prefer. Avoid talk radio or stations with a lot of news or commercials. Your dog may mistake the voices on the radio for those of live people talking inside or outside their homes. Note that I don't recommend leaving a television on, since this may provide too much visual stimulation for your dog.

- FROZEN PEANUT BUTTER TOY: Purchase an extra-thick and durable rubber dog toy that has an opening on one end, such as a Kong. Fill it with organic, unsweetened, creamy peanut butter. Put the peanut butter–filled toy in the freezer overnight. When you're about to leave the house, place the frozen toy inside your dog's crate. This will provide a nutritious snack for your dog while you're away and keep your dog entertained for hours.

## Tips for Crate-Training Your Dog

Make sure to leave your dog's crate out in the open and available at all times. Treat the crate as a piece of furniture that your dog will feel comfortable seeing and using on a full-time basis. You don't want the crate to be viewed as a punishment area, only seeing the light of day when your dog is going to the veterinarian or boarding kennel.

Although our schnauzers Buzz and Woody were already crate-trained when we adopted them and knew that's where they were to sleep at night, Dusty was only eight weeks old when she joined our family and had, understandably, not yet been introduced to sleeping in a crate. So, from her first night with us, she slept in a crate in between our pillows on our bed. With puppies, it's best to begin crate-training from the first night you bring them home.

With dogs who weren't crate-trained as a puppy, start slowly when introducing them to the crate. Allow them to investigate it beforehand as they would any other piece of furniture. Place them inside for a few minutes, talk to them, close the door, give them a treat through the closed door, open the door so they can exit, and praise them for doing a great job.

If you're training a dog to sleep in a crate at night or to remain in the crate when you leave the house for a few hours during the day, gradually increase the length of time they spend in the crate. At first, have them spend only a few minutes in the crate while you are present. Build up to ten minutes while you wait outside the room and out of sight. Once they get comfortable with being in the crate with you out of the room, put them in the crate, leave the house, and wait outside for fifteen minutes. Based on how well your dog responds to each increase of time in the crate and your being out of the house, work your way toward starting your car and driving around the block a few times. Next, drive to the store and shop for an hour. Next leave them in the crate while you are at work in the morning. Come back at lunchtime to check on them and let them out for a potty break.

If at any time your dog seems anxious or frightened upon entering the crate, go back to the last step they were comfortable with and gradually work your way toward the end goal of leaving them in the crate for a few hours at a time while you are away from home. It's important during all these steps to let your dog go at a pace they are comfortable with. View this as a positive experience for both of you and be confident that all will go well.

## Crate-Training for Cats

For cats, I suggest following a similar routine. You may not choose to leave your cat in a crate while you are out of the house or traveling, but there is no reason you can't if you choose. You may wish to do this if, for example, you have multiple cats in your household who don't always see eye to eye on things while unsupervised. Or you may have a cat who is not feeling well and needs some private time to recuperate. For that cat, spending time away from the other kitties in a crate might be a good thing. This will provide your cat with a safe haven where they can rest and be by themselves, and it's a better solution than placing your cat in a room with the door closed. Often cats will become anxious if they can hear activity happening outside the room they're in but can't see what's going on. This could lead to more undue stress on your cat.

I suggest leaving out your cat's crate, too, as a normal piece of furniture. You want your cat to realize that they can use their crate anytime they want to. Otherwise, if a cat crate is hidden in the closet and only brought out in situations that your cat doesn't enjoy, they will hide every time you get the crate out of the closet. Make their crate a fun and safe place for them at all times.

You should not to be afraid to travel with your cats on vacation, to a store, or around the block. So that they don't associate their crate with activities they don't like, take them to the veterinarian or groomer for no reason at all. Allow the veterinarian or grooming staff to pet and provide love, attention, and a few kitty treats to your cat while the cat is in the crate. Then close and secure the door to your cat's crate and take your cat home. This will reinforce with your cat that the crate is a positive place.

I wholeheartedly believe that, with proper training, crating dogs and cats is the way to go. It provides them with a dedicated sanctuary where they can go when you aren't at home, when everyone is sleeping, or when the household gets too chaotic or noisy. Some people I know feel that it would be cruel to lock their dogs and cats in a crate while they're gone. They want their dogs and cats to have free rein of the house. After all, it is the animals' house, too. Others I know can't be bothered with properly crate-training their dogs and cats or don't like a crate to be left out full-time. Based on my experience, they're missing the boat. Whether you're at home or traveling, a crate provides a safe environment for dogs and cats and should be viewed by all as a positive place.

# 22

# Making Outings Enjoyable

Going outside for a potty break, a walk, or a drive around town, or to simply to get out of the house for a while, should be enjoyable for us and our dogs. I have friends who like to drive around the neighborhood in their golf cart with their cats on leash or in a small cat carrier. They take them to the beach for a little sunbathing and fresh sea air. Yes, being part of nature is important for us, our dogs, and our cats alike. However, sometimes it becomes a major production to wrangle the dogs or cats and get them outside. Then, once you're out there, all the distractions and activity happening can be overwhelming to dogs and cats and turn what should be a pleasant experience into a stressful ordeal.

Dog owners often tell me that they hide their dog's leash in a drawer or behind the door until they are absolutely ready to go outside with their dog. Otherwise, if the dog sees the leash come out of the drawer or from behind the door too soon, they become overexcited. Some dogs pounce at the door trying to open it before everyone is ready, and others run around the house barking and howling until they finally see the door open. Once the door is open, whether they're on leash or not, they run out like escaped convicts from a prison or children exiting school on the last day before summer break. It can be stressful for us as well as our dogs.

Some of my clients' families have big fenced backyards for their dogs and cats to play in. This is great and always preferred over a smaller yard where there isn't enough room to adequately spread out. However, they tell me that even with the big backyard, their pets seem to get bored quickly when left alone outside. This leads to their pets getting into trouble like digging, climbing the fence, knocking open the gate, and chasing and killing the various wild critters that may visit the yard (more on this in chapter 24). So the people end up keeping a constant vigil on their dogs and cats or constantly worrying about the mischief they're getting into. The outdoor experience then becomes a stressful situation for all involved.

I've heard of this happening with cats as well. Clients have contacted me because their cats get too anxious when they want to go outside. Some cats will sit by the back door and vocalize in an almost crying manner until they are finally let out. Sometimes this happens in the early hours of the morning. One client stated that her cat would jump on the screen door to the back porch and hang on the screen mesh until the door was finally opened.

Those who live in big cities can't simply let their dogs out; they have no choice except to walk their dogs around the neighborhood. Often they have to navigate stairways, elevators, and all their neighbors who live in the building. Once outside, they have to maneuver around more people, cars, and bicycles and deal with all the noises that are customary in a big city. Some have told me that they look for every way possible to avoid walks and trips outside with their dogs because the experience is stressful for them as well as their dogs. I've even heard of people with small dogs placing grass turf or artificial grass on their balconies. When their dogs need to go potty or go outside for some air, they open the balcony door for the dog to go outside. Still others have told me they place piddle pads in their garage, storage area, or shower stall when their dog is too stressed to go outside.

In these cases I always suggest the following steps in order to curtail the stress that sometimes accompanies going outside.

- PREPARE: Make sure you have properly prepared for taking your dog outside. Regularly inspect leashes and collars to make sure that they're not frayed and that tags, buckles, and latches are secure. If you take your dog out on a leash, make sure the leash is easily accessible. Leave the leash out all the time so your dog can see it, rather than hiding it in a drawer or behind the door. Your dogs will get used to the leash being out and will not get as excited as they would if you kept it hidden and only took it out when it was time to go outside. If it's cold outside, make sure you have your coat and gloves on before proceeding to the door. If possible, take a peek out the window to see if there are any neighbors, workers, or other animals you might encounter outside. Do the same for your cats to make sure there aren't any unexpected surprises waiting for them outside.

- COMMUNICATE: Verbally communicate to your dogs and cats about what is going to happen, how you need them to act while outside, and why this will make it a pleasant experience for all. Communicate this information to them well before proceeding to the door. They need to know if it's going to be a short visit outside or if they will have a longer time to play, lounge, and investigate out there. They need to know that you would like for them to stay out of trouble and remain safe. Let them know if they are likely to encounter people or animals and that they should not be stressed about the situation. This will keep them informed about what is happening and how they should handle the situation and allow you to feel less stressed about allowing them to go outside or about being with them outside.

- RELEASE: Once you have prepared yourself and your dogs and cats for going outside, you can release any worry, fear, or negative energy that you have built up within your body. Take a breath, stay calm, and open the door to all that the outside world has to offer.

If possible, spend time with your dogs and cats during every visit outside as opposed to simply opening the door and letting them go out to explore the yard on their own. Help them stay focused on the reason for going outside in the first place, whether it's simply for a quick potty break or for them to keep you company while you do some yard work. Once you've all gone outside, if you verbalize again why you're outside with them, they'll stick to the task at hand. Also, use the time to get back in touch with nature, the world, and your dogs and cats. Going outside should be an enjoyable experience for you and your dogs and cats. Investigate and enjoy all the wonderful things the great outdoors has to offer. Just breathe, relax, and have fun!

# 23

## Walking on a Leash

We visit one of the many parks near our house every afternoon with our dogs. We find that our daily park walks provide our dogs the mental and physical stimulation they need to keep them healthy. As a matter of fact, the walks do the same thing for us. They provide a great opportunity to soak up some sunshine, breathe some fresh air, and get some exercise. Plus, they provide us with quality time with our dogs and allow us to forget about work and any other challenges going on.

We like to mix it up by visiting a different park each day. The dogs always know we are going to the park; they just don't know which one until we get a little closer to it. It really helps keep them mentally stimulated. We all seem to enjoy one particular park the most. That park is the closest to our home, which makes it easy to get to and allows us to spend more time exploring the actual park instead of riding in the car. It is also usually less populated than the others. There are some nicely paved walking paths, an open field to explore, a playground area with sand and mulch, two separate fenced dog-park areas, and a walking trail that winds through the woods and near a creek where we've seen people take their larger dogs to play and swim. The park offers more than enough opportunities to get exercise and sniff the surroundings.

While at the park, we always make sure our dogs are on a leash. First of all, it's the law in our county to keep dogs on a leash, except in areas designated specifically for dogs. Second, you never know when you're going to encounter a person or another dog who is not comfortable with you or your dogs. Some dogs are just not that social. Third, you never know when something is going to distract your dogs and cause them to run away unexpectedly. This particular park is especially known for the deer that inhabit the fields and surrounding woods. We've been lucky enough to see them grazing in the open fields on occasion. It would be easy for a dog to want to run off after the deer and then find himself lost or in trouble. Numerous clients have contacted me because their dog took off in pursuit of a squirrel, rabbit, chipmunk, or deer when walking off leash at a park or on a hiking trail. In each case, they have told me that their dog had never done this before.

One day, we were concluding our walk with our dogs at the park and returning to our car. As we approached the parking lot, we noticed a bright-red SUV pulling into a parking place. Once the SUV was parked, a woman wearing running gear got out of the vehicle and began running in our direction, making her way to the wilderness path. She stopped for a moment, turned toward her SUV and yelled, "Bernie!" Suddenly, a large yellow Labrador retriever appeared and was initially heading toward his owner. He had a collar on but wasn't on a leash. Once he saw us, he completely ignored the calls of his human companion, altered his course, and started to walk directly toward us. She smiled and yelled to us, "Don't worry. He's friendly!" to which I promptly yelled, "Well, my dogs aren't!" The smile quickly left her face as she rushed over to grab her dog by the collar. She then proceeded to pull her dog away until everyone was a safe distance from each other.

Neither of our dogs is aggressive toward people or other dogs, but nor are they totally comfortable meeting other dogs. Our toy schnauzer, Dusty, weighs a mere nine pounds. One wrong move, playful or not, from an unfamiliar, much larger dog could cause her real harm. Meanwhile, my miniature schnauzer, Kramer, is still learning to play nice with other people's dogs. When we adopted him, Kramer was not used to walking everywhere on a leash and had never visited a park until we started taking him with us to the park every day. He clearly hadn't been exposed to many other dogs before we adopted him. He is extremely gentle with Dusty but is sometimes unsure of other dogs when they approach. Because Kramer considers himself Dusty's self-appointed protector, he will position himself between Dusty and the approaching dog and bark at that dog until the dog has passed us. Of course, we continue to work on this with him by reminding him that while we appreciate his wanting to protect Dusty from unfamiliar dogs, that's our job and he should just enjoy his walk. Introducing dogs to each other should always be done gradually and in a controlled manner.

So my advice is not to assume that every dog is friendly just because you believe your dog is. Also, keeping your dogs on leash while in public will ensure their safety as well as the safety of other dogs and people they may encounter. If you want to let them off leash, take them to a secure area marked specifically for dogs for that purpose. But please keep in mind that, even in those settings, dogs will be dogs — they sometimes get rough when they play with one another, and unintentional injuries can occur. Plus, while your dog may listen well to you, you can't always anticipate another dog's actions should they approach you or your dog. Last, if you have a dog that weighs twenty pounds or less like both of my dogs, keeping your dog on leash while walking them outside is a deterrent to large birds of prey that have been known to quickly swoop down and carry off dogs of this size. So always use your best judgment when deciding whether to let your dog off leash, even in your own backyard or when permitted by law to do so.

If your dog shows signs of leash lunging and aggression, the first step is to stay calm. Try to identify a possible source of your dog's potential agitation long before they see it. You will then have the opportunity to alter your walking course or direction or prepare yourself for the introduction to the possible source of the frustration. Either way, continue to stay calm and positive. Communicate verbally with your dog that you see the person or animal and that it is okay. Distract them with a favorite treat, toy, or item that will turn their focus onto the item and not the person or animal. Praise them for letting you know that they saw the person or animal and let them know that they did a good job in handling the situation.

## Tips for Walking Your Dog on Leash

If your dog is new to walking on a leash or tries to pull you down the street, I suggest the following steps:

- START SMALL: Allow your dog to see the leash and investigate how it looks and smells. Leave it out so they can see it on a regular basis and get comfortable with it. Place the leash on your dog while you are in the house. Allow your dog to walk around for the day with the leash on in order to become comfortable with having it attached to their collar. Once you have accomplished this, try holding the leash and walking them inside the house. Work your way up to taking them on the porch or in your backyard with the leash on. While you are doing each of these steps, praise your dog for doing a great job, and don't forget to reward them with one or two small treats.

- PREVENT PULLING: If your dog tends to pull while walking, or to avoid injury to a puppy's trachea when you are training them on how to properly walk with you outside, you may want to utilize a harness-and-leash combination instead of just a leash attached to their collar. Others I've spoken with whose dogs tend to pull while on walks have high praise for the Gentle Leader Headcollar, although I have never used one with any of my dogs. Chest harnesses can also be very effective and easier to introduce dogs to. With Dusty and Kramer, my schnauzers, I use the combination of a Martingale dog collar and a leash when we're outside. Martingale dog collars are used for gentle control, unlike choke, pinch, or shock collars, which have been proven to harm dogs both physically and mentally regardless of whether they are used properly or not.

- COMMUNICATE AND VISUALIZE: Before going out for a walk in the neighborhood or park, communicate and visualize to your dog. Let him know what to expect during the walk, what he needs to do, and why this will be a good thing for both of you. Visualize the path you're going to be walking, how calm you both will be during the walk, how your dog will walk beside you and not pull you or lag behind, and how your dog will stay focused during the walk.

- STAY RELAXED AND CONFIDENT: Before heading out the door, take a deep breath and relax your body. Visualize the oxygen flowing through every part of your body and removing any doubt, worry, or fear that you may be holding on to. Start your walk with your dog on the inside part of the sidewalk, away from the traffic. This will help with the noise passing cars may make and keep your dog from trying to run into the street. Continue to relax, leaving a little slack in the leash. If your dog pulls, stop immediately and have him stay or sit. Allow the leash to be somewhat relaxed again before proceeding with your walk.

If your dog is doing a great job, let him know. Praising him throughout the walk and letting him know what to expect always helps with the walk. If you encounter someone walking toward you, or another dog being walked in the area, identify the situation early. Don't tense your body or start to fret. Instead, breathe, relax, and trust that all will be well and you'll continue your walk as planned. Communicate to let your dog know what the situation is, what he needs to do, and why this will be a good thing. Say something like "Yes, I see the person with their dog walking our way. I need you to be a sweet and calm dog so we can continue our walk. This will make me happy and will allow you to also enjoy our walk." Communicating this verbally, while visualizing a positive outcome, will help you and your dog to relax. However, if you notice that the approaching dog is not being restrained sufficiently by the owner or is acting in a way that makes you or your dog uncomfortable, you can cross to the other side of the street. Once you have passed the person and other dog, praise your dog for doing such great work.

## Walking Your Cat on a Leash

You may be asking yourself, "How can these methods be applied to me walking my cat on a leash? Doesn't this only pertain to dogs?" Well, walking on a leash can be good for you and your cat as well.

My friend Sally takes her cats out for walks and also allows them to ride with her on the golf cart. She has a special kitty harness with a short, thin leash that she puts on them before leaving the house. She walks her cats around the yard, around the neighborhood, and sometimes to the local beach. The cats are a little older and are easy to control on leash. Once they have the harness and leash on, they seem to be comfortable with the situation. She tells me that she's never seen them get anxious about going for walks and they seem to enjoy themselves while they are outside, as long as it's not for too long. After all, they live in Florida, and it can get quite hot there! She says people often come over to talk with her while she's out with her cats. Most smile and tell her they think it's pretty neat seeing a cat walking around outside on a leash. I'm sure they can't wait to get home to tell others about this unusual sight they've just seen!

For your cats, I recommend initially placing on the harness and leash while indoors. Do this for a few minutes per day for the first few days. If your cat handles this well, then gradually increase the length of time up to a couple of hours. If you have a screened porch or a deck, you can work with your cats on leash there. It will allow them to hear the noises from outside while still being in a protected environment. When you take your cat outdoors on leash for the first time, be sure to do so in a relatively quiet outdoor area where there aren't a lot of people or other animals around. Take your time and make sure both you and your cat are comfortable and confident before going to other outdoor areas where there are more people, neighbors' dogs, and vehicles driving by. Sometimes, the amount of activity outside your home can prove to be too much for a cat walking on a leash down the sidewalk.

Walking your dog and cat on a leash should be fun for everyone. It can provide great mental and physical stimulation for you, your dogs, and your cats. It's a great opportunity to bond with them, too. I encourage everyone to become comfortable with walking their dogs and cats on leash. Even if you have a big fenced yard, it's still important to take your animals for walks off the property. Going on walks provides everyone the opportunity to get out and about, check out the sites, and meet new friends along the way.

# 24

## Dogs and Cats in the Yard

Having a big yard for your dogs and cats to play in is the ideal scenario. While a fenced yard should not be your dog's or cat's only exposure to the outdoors (as mentioned in chapter 23), a fenced yard will provide them with physical and mental stimulation, which all dogs and cats need, and give them a safe and secure place to get exercise and be surrounded by nature.

If you're lucky enough to have a yard, take advantage of it! The yard is a great place to spend quality time with your dogs and cats. Here are some suggestions for activities to do with your dogs and cats in the yard:

- Work on your communication and visualization techniques with them.
- Play agility, fetch, or exercise games with them.
- Bring toys outside and hide them around the yard. Allow your pets to investigate and search for the hidden toys.

- Place treats around the railings of your porch or near fence posts and let your animals track them down. This is a fun way for them to use their strong sense of smell to find new treasures.
- Relax and unwind with them while lounging on a comfy chair. Take a good book outside to read and simply be in their calming space. Perhaps the book you'll read with them is this one!

## Keeping an Eye on Dogs and Cats in the Yard

A fenced backyard should be a safe haven for your dogs and cats to play in and simply be with one another. However, having a fenced yard doesn't mean you should simply leave your dogs or cats outside alone for long periods of time or for a full day. Many undesirable things could happen to them while they were left alone. Dogs who are regularly left alone for long periods in the backyard can become overly protective of their yard. This can lead to many challenges, including fence fighting with other dogs and excessive barking at people in neighboring yards or those simply walking by who are in view.

Without supervision, both dogs and cats can become bored with the lack of activity in the yard and get into mischief. For example, they can get distracted by other animals that may enter or be near the yard and try to chase or harm them.

I'm also familiar with cases in which a dog or cat was stolen right out of their yard. For example, my client Christine's dog was stolen from her back deck minutes after she let him out. Christine walked inside to grab some toys for him to play with, and when she returned, her dog was gone. Apparently, someone had been casing her house and looking for the perfect opportunity to steal her dog. So, when your animals are outside in the yard, be sure to check on them from time to time or, better yet, spend time out there with them.

## Keeping the Yard Safe and Secure

The yard should be secured with a fence around the perimeter so other dogs can't enter, one that is sturdy so the dogs can't bend or break through the fencing, and with secure gates that can't be pushed open when a dog jumps against them. I've been contacted more times than I can count by people whose dogs managed to escape from their fenced backyards. This often happens because a visitor opens a gate and accidentally lets out the dog or because they forget to close and lock the gate behind them. Sure enough, as soon as the dog is let outside, they run right toward the open gate and make their escape. Some dogs just explore the neighborhood and later return. Some dogs go missing for many days, and others never make their way back home. In the worst cases, the dog runs into the road and gets hit by a passing car.

Brenda contacted me because her dog, Lucas, had climbed over a six-foot wooden privacy fence. She was amazed that he had managed to get over such a tall fence. However, she hadn't realized that a plank on the fence had developed a rather large hole in it, which allowed Lucas to get a foothold and propel himself over the fence. Deer regularly roamed in the back wooded area behind the fence, and this always excited Lucas. He would run up and down the interior fence line and often try to climb the fence. On this occasion, he found the perfect spot to escape. Fortunately, a neighbor recognized Lucas and managed to capture and bring him home.

Another client, Sandy, had older, outdoor cats that she left in a fenced backyard while she was at work. Sandy would check in on the cats once she arrived home in the evening. Usually, the cats would lounge on the deck or in a custom-made treehouse in the middle of the yard. For years, nothing bad had happened, but one day Sandy arrived home and one of her cats was severely injured and needed to be rushed to the veterinarian's office. At first, she thought one of her other cats had attacked the injured cat. However, she noticed a suspicious orange clump of fur on the ground — all her cats were dark or gray in color and didn't have any orange markings. She came to find out that an unneutered stray cat was the culprit. Though her cats were unable to scale her tall, secure backyard fence, it hadn't stopped a stray cat from entering the yard.

Regularly check the security and maintenance of your yard while you're out there with your dogs and cats. Inspect the fenced area and gates to make sure they are secure and functional. Make sure no boards have come loose or holes have developed in the wood or metal fencing. Make sure no holes have been dug under the fence. Walk along the back decks where your cats spend time to make sure none of the adjacent window screens have holes in them and that the area is secure. Many types of foliage can be toxic to animals, so check that no loose limbs, debris, or unwanted foliage has fallen into the yard. Immediately after a maintenance person has visited the house, always check the area to make sure all gates are securely closed before releasing your dogs and cats. If you wait too long, you are liable to forget they were at the house.

Providing a regular maintenance check of your yard, fence, and property could prevent any accidental escapes by your pets and keep unwanted visitors out of your yard.

Use your big backyard as a place to better connect with your dogs and cats, while making sure their outdoor environment is secure.

# 25

## Digging Dogs and Cats

We all have heard stories of dogs taking a bone, running outside, and finding a nice, secure place to bury it. Certain breeds of dogs are notorious for digging holes in the ground or digging under fences. Hounds, like beagles, bassets, and bloodhounds, dig under fences to escape or to catch rodents on the other side. Terriers and dachshunds dig holes to hunt underground animals like rats and moles. Thick-coated dogs like huskies and Saint Bernards dig holes in order to lie in a cool spot on a hot day. Yet even some dog breeds that are usually not known for digging may dig holes in their yard or under fences.

My schnauzers have never dug a hole in the yard to bury a bone or a stick. They do, however, like to investigate all the holes that have been dug by the squirrels, chipmunks, moles, and other wildlife that have visited our Southern garden in the back of our house. They like to stick their noses in the holes to see if they can smell anything or get to the critter that created the hole. We are fortunate that none of the holes they have found have been near the actual fence line. Otherwise, I'm sure they would have worked harder to enlarge the hole and get to the other side.

My schnauzers like to dig imaginary holes in the bedding and blankets inside the house. They'll take a favorite treat, a chew bone, or a piece of food and run to the nearest doggy bed or comfortable blanket on the couch. They then proceed to dig furiously until the bedding or blanket is totally fluffed up to their liking. To avoid upsetting us or destroying anything, they make sure not to damage the items they are digging on. They then place the item gently in the middle of the fluff pile and then push the bedding or blanket with their noses until the item is no longer in view. If they catch us watching them in their digging-and-burying process, they will take the item to a different secure location and try it again.

As for the cats, they are notorious at digging in the outdoor planters that surround our house. It doesn't matter if the planter is nearly empty or full of dirt. If a plant is inside the planter, they will look for ways to nudge their bodies beside the plant, leaving just enough room for their bodies to be in the planter. Usually, they do this in order to find a new potty place. This is especially true if the potting soil is fresh. It smells good to them, and the loose soil is much easier to dig in. Sometimes, they have been known to help pat down the dirt while my wife, Kim, is busy planting new plants in the pots. They can be quite the green-paw gardeners.

## Pet Sandboxes

Although outdoor digging hasn't been a problem in my family, numerous clients have contacted me over the years seeking a way to stop their dogs from digging in unwanted areas. I had a client whose Jack Russell terrier, Spike, was a notorious digger at their back fence. As soon as she let Spike out the back door to potty or play, he would head toward the back fence area. His favorite spot was the far right-hand corner of the fence. Sometimes he dug because he could hear other animals, such as deer and squirrels, on the other side of the fence. But most of the time he did it out of pure habit. It was a calming method for him, and he saw no problem in what he was doing. He never managed to dig completely under the fence to escape. He dug just enough to tear up the lawn and cause a mess on his paws and nails. So I recommended that she place a sandbox in the corner that Spike could dig in. She had her husband build the sandbox, placed some children's play sand inside, hid a few of Spike's favorite toys, partially covered with sand, in the sandbox, and showed it to Spike. Spike immediately took to it and now chooses his sandbox as his favorite place to dig.

Sandboxes have been loved by children for generations. They provide a safe and dedicated area where a child can play in the sand, dig holes with their favorite play trucks and shovels, and bury items as if they were a pirate's treasure. If kids love to play in sandboxes, why wouldn't your dog?

You can build your dog's sandbox by nailing together four evenly sized pieces of wood. Or, if you don't want to build the sandbox yourself, you can use an old, large tractor tire (this works best for smaller dogs) or purchase a premade plastic or resin sandbox.

Make sure to place the sandbox away from the fence line. Also, if there is already a favorite place that your dog has dug, then place the sandbox there. Fill it at least halfway with sand, wood chips, or loose dirt, making sure it is deep enough that it would be difficult for your dog to dig in the ground below. To get your dog's attention and help him associate the box with a positive reward, partially bury some favorite toys and nonedible bones inside the box and let your dog find and rebury the items. Keep things fresh by introducing new or different toys and bones on occasion.

Communicate to your dog that this is the place he should dig if he wants to. Visualize this as his only digging location and see him using it exclusively for digging. Make digging a positive experience for both of you.

Although cats don't typically like to dig for the same reasons as dogs, you can create a designated area in your yard for this purpose for your cats. You may want to make the area smaller, depending on the number of cats who like to dig. Also, if your cat likes to dig in your existing planters, you can also add one or two extra-large biodegradable planters around your deck, back porch, or yard. Your cats can dig in them and go potty in them, and when the planters deteriorate, you can simply throw them away. Make sure to communicate what this dedicated digging space is to be used for and visualize them using this location exclusively.

If a pet sandbox is not appropriate for your backyard or you're looking for other things to distract your dog from digging you can play hide-and-seek with your dog. Hide-and-seek is a great game to keep your dog distracted and mentally stimulated. Before allowing your dog in the yard, place a few favorite toys and treats in strategic locations in the yard. You can place the toys and treats near fence posts, under the front side of a deck or porch, under a tree or bush, or anywhere in the yard where it is safe and your dog will stay out of trouble.

Each time you play hide-and-seek, you can mix it up a little to keep the search fresh. Find new places to hide the toys and treats. Also, change the types of toys and treats that you place in the yard. Keeping things fresh and fun will go a long way in deterring your dog from digging.

# 26

## Show Dogs

I have attended and spoken at many kennel club events and meetings over the years. It's always fascinating to talk with owners and breeders of beautiful show dogs. Some clubs are breed-specific and others have a wide array of breeds. The groups are passionate about the dogs, the shows, and the numerous show competitions and related events. The members work daily, training their dogs for specific competitions and often traveling great distances to attend events. Some fly with their dogs to out-of-town events, but most drive. They load their trucks, vans, and motor homes with their dogs and all their training and show-related items. They stay at motels with their dogs during the event or simply settle in at the event's designated show locations and stay in their mobile homes or campers. To me, it's a fascinating lifestyle and one that I'm constantly learning more about.

Rick had a national short-distance champion border collie, DJ, who he had worked with for a number of years. In a short-distance event, sometimes referred to as toss-and-fetch or throw-and-catch, contestants have a predetermined amount of time, usually sixty seconds, to throw a disc as many times as possible on a field marked with increasingly longer distances. The dogs are awarded points for catches based on the distance of each throw. When the dog retrieves the disc in midair, they receive extra points. Only one disc is used for each dog during the event. It is critical for the dog to retrieve the disc, run back to their human partner, deliver the disc, and run back out into the field to retrieve the disc again. For Rick and DJ, this was never an issue — until recently. DJ decided that he was happy to retrieve the disc and return to his human partner — but he did not want to release the disc. Instead, he wanted to turn it into a tug-of-war game. This change in behavior cost them both a recent championship. It was up to me to determine why DJ had suddenly changed his behavior and to come up with a solution.

After a brief chat with DJ, I uncovered that he was tired of having the disc quickly removed from his mouth. He still liked running, jumping, and retrieving the disc. But he wasn't happy that the disc was sometimes taken from his mouth somewhat forcefully. I informed Rick of this, and he was shocked. He had had no idea DJ felt this way. They had followed the same routine for years, and it seemed to be working well. He had to remove the disc from DJ's mouth as quickly as possible in order to throw it again. Time was of the essence for a short-distance competition. So we set forth the following plan to make sure everybody was happy and they would once again succeed in the competition.

- VISUALIZING THE PLAN: I had Rick sit quietly with DJ thirty minutes before each event. I asked him to visualize the process of the competition from the beginning of their scheduled time until the end: the disc in his hand; his long and perfect throw; DJ running, jumping, and catching the disc perfectly; DJ retrieving the disc and returning it promptly, releasing the disc into his hand; and repeating the entire process. A lot of great athletes use this form of visualization. Before a game, match, or tournament, they mentally prepare for their success by visualizing the complete event happening exactly how they want it to.

- COMMUNICATING THE DESIRED RESULT: I asked Rick to verbally communicate to DJ what was about to happen at the event and what he needed from DJ in order to succeed. I asked him to share with DJ why this was important and why it would be a good thing for both of them. I asked him to begin using the keyword "easy" when DJ returned the disc to him. I suggested that instead of taking the disc quickly from DJ's mouth, he should place his hand out with his palm up and allow DJ to gently place the disc in Rick's hand. I reassured him that it would not take any additional time and DJ would be more forthcoming when leaving him with the disc.

- FEELING CONFIDENT: I asked Rick to feel confident that this was going to work. If he allowed any doubt or fear into the process, the plan would fail. But if he followed the plan and projected confidence, I knew they would succeed.

A few months later, Rick contacted me with the results. They had followed the plan to a tee and remained confident of its success. Sure enough, DJ was a national champion again!

Many other clients with whom I've consulted have used this process with dogs they are showing at dog shows. Another client's dog always showed well in the local and regional conformation dog shows but fell short of winning his category in those shows. In a conformation dog show, judges compare dogs based on what they believe represents the breed's ideal standard — assessing their coat, features, attitude, and overall appearance — and on how the dogs are handled by the people showing them. Sometimes the handler is the dog's owner but often it's someone the dog works with specifically for the show. My client Susan always handled her own dog. Susan's dog, a whippet named Bailey, passed through the event with flying colors except for the presentation of his tail. Each time Bailey entered the show area, he would tuck his tail instead of presenting it proudly, as whippets are expected to do during these competitions. This cost him points, and they always fell short of winning the event.

After a brief chat with Bailey, I uncovered that he didn't know he was supposed to keep his tail raised during the competition. It was natural for him to leave his tail relaxed when he was at home, and he figured he could do the same at the event. He wasn't lowering his tail out of fear of being at the event, which is what Susan had assumed. It was just that the importance of the erect tail had never been communicated to him.

I explained to Susan what Bailey had shared with me, and she started to laugh. Sure enough, she had never told him what he needed to do with his tail during the competition. So she started visualizing the plan, communicating what Bailey needed to do, especially with his tail, and feeling confident before entering the show floor. I'm happy to report that Bailey is now winning his events with his tail held high.

# 27

## Equal Treatment

No matter how much we try to deny it, we all have favorites in our families. We have a favorite uncle that we always enjoy being around. We have a favorite parent with whom we seem to have a closer relationship. Our parents have a favorite child — as much as they don't want to admit it. And yes, we have favorite dogs and cats in our lives, too. We try not to talk about it much, feeling like we are bad people if we show favoritism between the animals in our family. Of course, we love every one of them. We attempt to show each of them the same amount of attention and divvy out the same amount of love. However, no matter how much we try to deny it, there is always one dog or cat with whom we have a stronger connection.

Susan had two cats, Puss and Boots, who she adopted as kittens when she was single and living in an apartment. It was not uncommon for the cats to lounge on the couch or chairs in the living room during the day and sleep with her in bed each night. After many years of living alone with the cats, Susan married Jim. He had a black Labrador retriever mix named

Rufus who was accustomed to sitting with Jim on the couch while he watched television and sleeping with him in bed.

Rufus was a gentle dog and never had any issues with Susan or her cats. Susan was not raised with dogs and didn't realize that dogs, too, like to lie on the couch and sleep in the bed. Susan kept Rufus on the floor or on his dog bed when resting or sleeping. Rufus's every attempt to join the family on the couch or in bed was rebuffed by Susan. Jim went along with what Susan wanted. This was just one of the many changes involved in bringing their two families together under one roof, and he trusted that all would work out in the end because he saw how much Susan cared about Rufus's well-being.

After a time, Rufus became anxious and restless when the rest of the family sat on the couch to watch television or went to bed each night. His constant pacing back and forth became too much for Susan to bear. Susan contacted me to determine why Rufus was pacing so much. After I communicated with him, he explained that he didn't understand why he couldn't join the rest of the family on the couch or sleep with them in bed. Susan hadn't realized the impact this was having on Rufus. So she decided to place a special throw blanket on one end of the couch and another at the foot of the bed so that Rufus could join them in these areas. Rufus was thrilled! He was finally able to join the rest of the family on the couch or in bed and the pacing stopped.

In our family, our little toy schnauzer, Dusty, is definitely a daddy's girl. She loves spending time with me and she is always close at hand. I was the first to hold her as a puppy, and I still carry her when she needs to go down the long and steep stairs at our house. I also carry her to her doggy car seat that's securely fastened in our truck. Dusty is always playful, which matches my personality to a tee. When she isn't harassing her "brother," Kramer, to play, she is usually harassing me to play. Virtually no matter what I do and where I go, Dusty is close at hand.

To make sure Dusty receives equal attention from both of us, my wife, Kim, walks Dusty while we're at the park. Dusty loves to investigate every little thing at the park. The only time she runs is to catch up with me or with Kramer when she sees that he's found something that has caught his interest. She takes her time to explore the wonders of everything around her.

Kramer is definitely a momma's boy. He bonded with Kim from day one, refusing to leave her side. Virtually all dogs and cats warm up to me immediately, and many come running toward me when I enter the room. But our boy Kramer actually took his time before warming up completely to me and allowing me to be his main belly-rubbing partner. I guess he figured that I already had a dog in Dusty, so his momma needed a dog to call her own.

During our daily park time with the dogs, we change it up a little. Kramer loves to run and can't wait to get going. He also loves to explore the trails at the park and go tromping through the woods every chance he can. We call him our "wood" dog, as he loves nothing better than to spend his time exploring the woods.

Even though you may have a stronger emotional connection with one animal in your household than the others, it's important to spend dedicated time with each of them. Finding things to do together that you have in common and spending that quality time together is rewarding for both of you. For example, switch from spending time with one dog to another during playtime, walks, and explorations. Get to know your other animal's personality and energy a little better. This will help you to better understand their wants and needs. In return, your dogs will get to know your personality and energy better and will gain a better understanding of your wants and needs. This way, you will have the best relationship possible with each of them.

This is equally important with your cats. You need to understand each of their personalities and energies, wants and needs. The best way to do this is to spend time with them as a group and individually. Do more than just feed them and look after their physical needs — also make time for play, exercise, and opportunities to experience new things together.

In our family, I'm usually the one who looks after the cats. The routine is for each of them to greet me and follow me to their food dishes each morning. I ask each of them individually how they are doing and what they have planned for the day. I let all of them know what to expect outside regarding the weather, and inform them if I have plans to leave that day. I inform them if guests will be visiting or any workers will be at the house. I then ask them to stay near our house and to be safe if they go off to explore.

To keep things fresh and interesting, Kim occasionally cares for the cats, instead of letting me always do it. She feeds them at night or on the weekends and spends time with them planting plants in the various pots around the house. They always find this fascinating, since she doesn't get to visit with them or work in her gardens or planters unless it's a day off work or on the weekend. Because she is performing tasks for the cats that I usually perform on weekdays, she makes sure to follow the same routine that I do when I interact with them.

She greets each of the cats individually. She asks each of them separately how they are doing and what they did during the day (or will be doing, as applicable). She provides them with the latest weather forecast and tells them her plans for the day. She lets them know of any guests or workers that will be arriving at the house. Last, she tells them to stay close to the house and to be safe.

Treating all your dogs and cats equally is important in order to have a peaceful and happy house. We all have our favorites, but we won't tell them that. Instead, share your attention and love equally, and they will do the same.

# 28

## Company Is Coming

Sometimes the arrival of company causes cats and dogs to get anxious or unsettled. But you can take proactive measures to manage the situation and prevent any upheaval.

Vanessa had a calico cat named Precious and a schipperke dog named Spirit. Precious got along extremely well with Spirit and the rest of the family. She spent most of her days basking in the sunshine while lounging on the window ledge. Spirit was a quiet dog and simply loved spending time playing with Vanessa. Nothing in the world seemed to bother either of the animals until visitors arrived at the house. As soon as someone rang the doorbell, Spirit would go into a barking frenzy. Even after the visitors had been greeted and escorted into the house, Spirit would continue to bark. Sometimes he became so stressed that Vanessa would have to let him outside in his fenced backyard until he calmed down. Once he was noticeably calmer, Vanessa would bring Spirit back inside. Precious reacted to visitors by running upstairs and hiding under the bed until the visitors left. Until she talked with me about the situation, it never occurred to Vanessa that she could have avoided much of the drama and stress by simply communicating to Precious and Spirit ahead of time.

From that point forward, Vanessa made it a point to let Precious and Spirit know when visitors would be coming over, how long they would be there, that she wanted them to help her make the guests feel welcome by visiting with them, too, and that this would make the event fun for everyone. Communicating with them in this way proved very beneficial to all involved whenever visitors came to their home.

When Kim and I know that our friends are coming over for a visit, we ask them to slowly pull into our driveway and take a quick look around for the cats. On most occasions, they will find one of our semi-feral cats lying in the driveway. Usually, it's Momma Kitty, since she rarely strays from our property. We also ask them to make their way down the driveway slowly while keeping an eye out to see if Momma Kitty or any of the other cats are lying beneath the Leland cypress trees, near the various bushes around the side of the house, or under their favorite cherry tree, all of which border our driveway.

Our cats don't seem to mind some visitors being at our house, but they remove the welcome mat for others. For the most part, they pay little attention to the arrival of the postal delivery person, mostly because she usually leaves the packages by the mailbox located at the end of the driveway. But even when she occasionally places a package on our front porch, it doesn't interrupt the cats' routines, since they rarely visit the front porch unless it's later at night. The UPS and FedEx delivery drivers are a different story. They'll pull up at the end of the drive, let their diesel engines idle, open and close a series of doors, and walk quickly down the driveway toward the house.

The noise of the truck and the smell of the diesel fumes are too much for the cats to handle, let alone a strange person walking quickly down the driveway carrying a box or package. They hear the noise, smell the smell, take one last look, and hightail it to the woods behind our house. Once the noise, smell, and unfamiliar person have left our property, they cautiously emerge from their hiding places and resume their usual lounging and grooming routines.

Though I inform our cats every Saturday that the landscapers will be visiting a couple of hours later, all but Momma Kitty waste no time in departing. As I turn to walk away, they scurry away from the yard. They want no part of the mowers, Weedwackers, or grass blowers. The landscape crew has always been nice to them the few times they've seen them, but the cats definitely don't want any part of that activity. Momma Kitty usually retreats into the garage and stays there until the landscapers leave. But we don't see the other kitties again until the landscapers are gone.

## Preparing Dogs for the Arrival of Guests

USE KEYWORDS AND VISUALIZATION: When introducing your dogs to people who are visiting your house, I recommend that you use similar positive keywords and visualizations as you do when introducing them to people outside of the home (see pages 96–97). However, dogs are generally more protective at their homes. They can also become too excited and lose focus on how to properly greet the visitor.

LET THE DOGS KNOW AHEAD OF TIME: When I know in advance that visitors are coming over, regardless of whether

Dusty and Kramer have met them or not, I always let the dogs know what is about to happen. Within thirty minutes of the guests' expected arrival I explain to my dogs who is coming for a visit, how I want them to handle the situation, and why they will enjoy it. At first they become excited but then quickly calm down to listen to everything I have to say, and then they relax until the guests arrive.

Introduce in a "Neutral Area": I also recommend introducing your dogs to guests in a "neutral area" of the home. A neutral area could be the fenced backyard area, the garage with the door open, on a leash in the front yard, or any other location that is not located directly inside the house and behind a closed door. Arranging to meet guests in a neutral area is less threatening for the dog and prevents any startling surprises, such as the doorbell ringing or someone walking in unannounced. Often I also ask our visitors to call us once they have arrived in the driveway rather than ringing the doorbell. This provides us with ample time to gather ourselves and head to the neutral zone.

Once everyone is in the neutral area we wait until the dogs calm down before the official greeting and petting begin. I often slip our guests a little treat or two. They can then ask the dogs to sit before giving them the treat. This allows the dogs to calm down further, focus their attention on receiving their treat, and then receive their reward for doing a good job. I then ask the dogs to show our guests inside to their home, and we all follow the dogs inside. (These are generally the only times the dogs enter the house before we do.)

Communicate with your dogs and cats in advance when you are planning on having guests over to visit. Let them know who is coming, what they need to do, and why this will be a fun occasion for everyone. Let them know when your friends arrive and remind them what you need from them and why this will be a good thing for them. Make the visit enjoyable for everyone instead of letting it become stressful and generating negative energy.

# 29

## Baby Is Here

One of the most exciting times in any family's life is the day when they bring home a new baby. The excitement of starting a life with a new baby girl or boy is thrilling for everyone. It can also be a time of great stress and drama, as there is so much to do and so many routines that need to be adjusted. In all the excitement of the new baby arriving, it can be easy to forget about the impact this will have on your dogs and cats. There will be one more person in the house that needs attention, care, and feeding. Not to mention the baby's unpredictable schedule — your dogs and cats can forget all about their present routines, at least for the foreseeable future. They will need to adapt their schedules to accommodate the new baby, just as you will have to adjust your schedule. This can cause a lot of emotional stress on your dogs and cats if not handled properly.

My wife, Kim, experienced this situation when she was young. Early on, when her parents brought her new baby sister home, they had not communicated to their seal point Siamese cat, Little Bit, about what was about to happen. I'm sure Little Bit sensed that something was about to change in the family. However, Kim was an older child when they had brought Little Bit home as a kitten. Little Bit had never experienced a baby being in her home. She definitely was not prepared for a baby who would be living in her house and demanding so much attention.

One day they lay Kim's baby sister, Jeannie, in her crib for her nap. They left the room and went downstairs for some rest and food, with the door partially open so they could hear her if she started crying. Everything was going fine, and not a peep out of the baby. After an hour, Kim's mom decided to go back upstairs to check on the baby. She looked into the room and saw Little Bit standing in the crib next to the child, sniffing her face. This startled Kim's mom, as she was unsure of what Little Bit was about to do. She feared the worst and ran quickly to the crib and shooed Little Bit out of the room. This was the first face-to-face exposure that Little Bit had with the baby, and I think she was simply puzzled as to what this little person was all about and why she smelled different from her other human companions. I'm sure she jumped into the crib to check everything out and really was not going to cause any harm. However, she wasn't supposed to be in the crib and that close to the baby. Kim's parents feared she would accidentally bite or scratch the baby. After this encounter, Little Bit never went back into the crib or near the baby when she was sleeping.

Some thirty years later, my wife's sister, Jeannie — the baby who Little Bit had jumped into the crib with — came to visit us. She was many months pregnant with her first child. One evening, she went to the guest bedroom and was preparing to go to bed. Our schnauzer Woody wanted to enter the room and spend some time with her before bedtime. Kim asked Jeannie if this was acceptable, and Jeannie agreed. Upon entering the bedroom, Kim put Woody up on the bed with Jeannie. He went over to her, sniffed her stomach, looked at Kim, and began to "whoo-whoo-whoo" repeatedly. Woody had always been a sensitive boy and could pick up on changes in energy. In this case, he picked up on the fact that Jeannie was carrying extra energy, her baby, and he was unsure what that was all about. We had neglected to explain to him that she was pregnant, never considering that Woody would sense the additional energy signature. It did not matter to Woody that the baby hadn't been born yet. He just felt the additional energy and was confused about what it was and where it was coming from.

Kim sat down on the bed beside her sister and Woody and explained to him what was going on — that her sister was carrying a baby in her stomach, that the baby was waiting to be born, and that this was the additional energy he was feeling. She asked him to be gentle and calm. She explained what a good thing this was and how happy everyone was about it. Woody immediately calmed down, listened, sniffed Jeannie's stomach a few times, and then was happy. During the rest of the visit, Woody didn't have any further "whoo-whoo-whoo" outbursts or pay much attention to the additional energy in the room.

## Tips for Introducing a Baby into the Household

Here's my advice for preparing your pets for the arrival of a new baby.

COMMUNICATE EARLY: As soon as you learn of the pregnancy, begin communicating to your dogs and cats. Believe it or not, some clients have told me that their dogs and cats started acting excited and became overly clingy long before they had even confirmed that they were pregnant. The animals were already sensing the new energy that was present in the house. Let your dogs and cats know when you become pregnant or when you plan to adopt a new baby. Explain to them that you will need them to be calm and gentle around the baby. Let them know that the baby will be one more person who will love them and play with them in the future. Let them share in your excitement.

COMMUNICATE FREQUENTLY: Before the baby arrives, keep your dogs and cats informed and involved. Let them see and sniff all the new baby furniture, clothes, blankets, and formula, and the endless supply of diapers you're bringing home. Verbally communicate with them that these items are for the baby. Use a keyword like "gentle" each time you handle one of the baby's items. Praise them for doing a good job while they're gently investigating the baby's items. Do this each time you handle the items or bring something new for the baby into the house. After a while, your dog or cat will know that these items are not theirs and they'll act indifferent toward them. This will keep them involved along the way, and the baby gear will be commonplace by the time the baby arrives.

INTRODUCE THEM EARLY AND CAREFULLY: Make sure the dogs and cats are among the first to greet the baby when you bring him or her home. Allow them to approach the baby while the baby remains in your arms. At first, they may not be eager to meet the baby because of the high energy coming from you as a result of your excitement to have the baby home. But eventually your pets will want to see what all the fuss is about. Allow your dogs and cats to spend time in the same room with the baby as long as you're there to supervise. At first, to get everyone comfortable being around each other, limit the exposure to those times when the baby is nursing or sleeping in your arms. You wouldn't want your animals' first exposure to the new baby to be a time when he or she is crying uncontrollably. The baby's distress not only would change your energy but may cause your animals to be hesitant about interacting with the baby.

KEEP THINGS CLEAN: Be careful that the baby not be exposed to any germs or allergens that your dogs and cats may bring into the room with them. Strategically place plenty of sanitary wipes throughout the house so that you can wipe off your hands if you pet your animals or they lick your hands while you are holding your baby. Dust the places where your baby plays, sits, or lies if your pets have been in those areas, and replace the baby's linens as often as necessary.

STAY INVOLVED: Keep your dogs and cats involved with everything that is happening in the house. It will take weeks or months to get anything close to a routine in place. Assign your dogs and cats jobs to do while you are tending to the baby's needs. Have them walk with you to get more formula or milk from the kitchen. Have them supervise the endless diaper changes. Have them keep your spot warm by lying on your side of the couch or bed. Dogs and cats love jobs and love to be informed. You might as well keep them involved and praise them for doing such great work.

DON'T WORRY: Clients often contact me worrying about how their dogs and cats are handling the new baby being around.

They worry that the dogs and cats are depressed and feel a lack of love and attention from them. Though it is important to provide your dogs and cats with love and attention, don't beat yourself up if you slip. If you continue to communicate with your dogs and cats, they will understand. They will be patient with you and know that you still love and care for them. Remember, they don't deal with human ego emotions like hate, spite, or resentment. They will be happy when they do receive love and attention from you, of course, even if it isn't on the same old schedule.

Susan and Jim were within a month of their expected due date of their new baby girl. Things were understandably very hectic at this stage, and they found it more difficult to maintain their normal schedules. Susan wasn't able to walk their golden retriever, Spike, as easily or as often as she had before she was pregnant. That responsibility now fell mostly on Jim to do before and after work.

Their normal routine had been for Susan to walk Spike a couple of additional times during the afternoon. Since Susan worked from home, walking Spike in the afternoon had never been a challenge and proved to be a nice break for both of them.

Spike, a gentle and playful dog, loved to carry his favorite toys around the house and greet people at the door with them. Spike would get restless, though, when he didn't receive enough attention or get to expend his excess energy during his frequent walks. Both Susan and Jim were concerned about how Spike would handle things once they brought the baby home. They knew the routine would become more chaotic, likely resulting in less playtime and walks with Spike. They were also concerned that Spike may think the baby was a new play toy or would try to mouth the baby like he did with his favorite toys.

I suggested that Susan and Jim start talking with Spike about the baby immediately and not wait until they brought her home. Spike knew things were already changing but didn't fully understand why. I suggested they pick a keyword like "gentle" to use exclusively when Spike would be near the baby or any of the baby's items. I also suggested they tell Spike that the baby would arrive in about a month and live with them from that point forward, that he would need to be gentle around the baby, and that this would make everyone happy.

I reminded them to visualize the positive outcome they were expecting. I also asked them to show some of the baby's items to Spike now and use the keyword while doing so. They needed to praise Spike when he left the item alone and thank him for doing such great work. I suggested that once the baby arrived, they allow Spike to spend supervised time near her and continue to use the keyword they had chosen.

A month later, they brought their new baby, Abby, home from the hospital. They slowly introduced Spike to Abby, used the word "gentle" whenever he approached her or investigated any of her baby items, visualized the desired outcome, and remained calm and confident during those times. Spike took to the situation like a champ! He never tried to take any of the baby's items as his own play toys. Instead, he often presented his favorite toys to Abby. He would sit next to Abby's crib, changing station, or rocking chair while she was there and never approached her or tried to mouth her. He even left the baby bottle, full of formula, alone when it occasionally fell to the ground.

The arrival of a new baby is an exciting and happy occasion for everyone. As long as you communicate with your dogs and cats, they will be equally excited and happy. Plus, eventually they will have a new play partner.

# 30

## A New Pet Has Arrived

Bringing home a new dog or cat is an exciting event in the lives of all animal lovers. Whether you bring home a puppy, a kitten, or an adult dog or cat, the excitement and thrill are the same. You are adding a new furry family member to your household to love and enjoy forevermore. Your new dog or cat is getting a new loving family and comfortable home to live in. Things can't get any better for everyone — except possibly the dogs and cats who already reside in the household. Did anyone remember to consider how the new furry addition would affect them?

The arrival of a new dog or cat can be stressful for the existing dogs and cats in the home. It's even more stressful for them if no one informs them in advance about what is happening and that the new dog or cat will be staying permanently. All kinds of questions enter the existing dogs' and cats' minds. For example: Who is this new animal? Will they be replacing me with this new animal? Will I receive the same amount of attention, love, and food? Will the new animal take over my favorite sunbathing spot or my bed? The list of questions they have can be endless.

Bringing home a new dog or cat without involving the existing furry family members can lead to disaster. The animals will be fighting for position and attention in the family hierarchy. Boundaries will be tested to see what the new dog or cat can get away with and what will not be tolerated by the other animals. All of this can lead to the animals fighting among themselves or simply not wanting to have anything to do with one another.

We experienced this early on when we considered adopting another dog, Marcie. A local rescue group had been fostering Marcie, and my wife, Kim, fell in love with her when she met her at one of my book-signing events. Marcie was an incredibly sweet, quiet, and gentle miniature schnauzer who curled up in Kim's lap the first time she met her. Marcie was well behaved and house trained, and never had any confrontations with the other foster dogs. She was submissive by nature and had no desire to become the dominant dog in anyone's family.

A volunteer brought Marcie over for a home visit and to see how she would interact with our two existing schnauzers, Buzz and Woody. Within five minutes of placing Marcie on the kitchen floor, commotion ensued. Woody started to bark, howl, and growl at her. Buzz, in order to ensure that neither Marcie nor Woody got hurt, positioned himself between the two dogs in an effort to run block between them. It didn't take long to realize that this was not going to be the right family dynamic for Marcie, Buzz, Woody, or us. We spent the next half hour talking to Woody to calm him down.

In our excitement about potentially adding Marcie to our

family, we had made the mistake of bringing her into our home without first talking to Buzz and Woody about it and fully explaining the situation. Woody was feeling all types of emotions and having numerous thoughts, and we had to reassure him that all was well. It didn't help matters that he couldn't see what was going on because he had lost his sight to sudden acquired retinal degeneration syndrome (SARDS) a year or so earlier. So, between our forgetting to talk with him ahead of time, the presence of an unfamiliar dog in his house, and his not being able to see, he reacted accordingly.

We learned from our mistake and set forth a plan for the next dog who would possibly become part of our family. After Buzz and Woody passed away, we adopted Dusty, a toy schnauzer. She was a puppy and we knew that we would have our hands full for a while. So we allowed her first year to be exclusively with us and no other dogs. This allowed all of us to establish our routines and Kim and me to enjoy puppy playtime and enough free time that at least one of us could do something else while the other tended to the demands of the new puppy.

As we approached Dusty's first birthday, we decided to consider adding another dog to our family. We knew that another dog would have to allow Dusty to rule the roost and be in control. She is a very feisty little dog and insists on being the boss. Since she is petite, weighing only nine pounds, we had to make sure to find a gentle dog who would not accidentally hurt her when they played or constantly chase her. We also wanted to make sure the first and any subsequent introductions would be pleasant for both dogs. We didn't want Dusty's focus to be solely on guarding her house, toys, and food. So we chose a neutral location for the introduction: our fenced backyard.

We made sure to communicate with Dusty in advance to

let her know that a dog was coming over to visit with us. We explained to her that she needed to feel comfortable with the dog and show her how things were done at our house. We made sure to tell her that the dog wouldn't come to live with us unless she agreed to it. We visualized the whole process before the new dog arrived and made sure that we all felt calm and positive about the introduction.

A volunteer from a local rescue organization brought the female miniature schnauzer over for a visit. She was six months old, full of energy, and already a little taller than Dusty. As soon as the new dog entered the backyard, we knew this was not going to be the right fit. The new dog was too playful with Dusty and constantly wanted to chase her. Thankfully, we knew to keep both of them on leash to maintain some degree of control over the situation. It was clear that Dusty wasn't comfortable with the new dog, and neither were we. However, introducing them in a neutral outdoor area proved to be a great way for them to meet. There was nothing to distract Dusty, and she didn't have to worry about defending her house.

A few weeks later we introduced Kramer, a fifteen-month-old male miniature schnauzer, to Dusty. We chose the same backyard location for the introduction and spent a few hours on a sunny Saturday afternoon with both dogs getting to know each other. We spent the first hour in the backyard allowing Dusty and Kramer to interact. It was obvious that Dusty was more receptive to Kramer than she had been with the first, younger schnauzer she'd met. We found out from Kramer's foster family that he was by nature a patient and gentle dog. That temperament came in handy when Dusty started playing with him and trying to wrestle with him. Kramer seemed to like Dusty, or he at least tolerated her crazy antics. He's a sensitive boy, and we could tell that he was unsure about everything that was going on.

Because the first hour in our backyard had gone so well, we felt comfortable bringing Dusty and Kramer into our screened-in back porch and removing their respective leashes. The hour we spent there also went well, so we decided to take both dogs inside. Of course, we asked Dusty to lead the way and show Kramer "her" house. He followed Dusty's lead and began to check out the living room, kitchen, and hallways. Everything seemed to meet with his satisfaction, and Dusty appeared comfortable with Kramer being in the house. After an hour inside, we all felt that Kramer would be a great fit for our family, but we wanted to talk about it a little more and make sure Dusty was okay with this decision, too. Within a couple of hours, we called his foster family and said we wanted to adopt Kramer into our family.

The next day, Kramer arrived with his foster mom. At first when they came inside, Dusty wasn't as welcoming. There was other activity going on in the garage that I had to attend to. So, between Dusty not knowing where I was and Kramer coming straight into our house through the garage entry door, Dusty was a bit out of sorts. Thankfully, Dusty's less-than-welcoming behavior didn't alter our decision to adopt Kramer. We all agreed that it would work out fine once everything settled down.

Kramer has now been with us for more than a year, and he and Dusty get along extremely well. In fact, he looks after her like he's her big brother when we go out for walks. If he gets too far ahead of her while we're out walking, he doubles back to make sure she's okay. Or if she barks and he can't see her because he's gotten too far ahead, he immediately comes running back toward her to make sure she's okay.

## Cat Introduction Success Story

Tanya contacted me regarding her cat being introduced to her fiancé's cats for the first time. They were scheduled to be married in a few months when they realized that all the cats had not been introduced to one another. The plan was for Tanya and her cat to move into her fiancé's house after they were married. She was concerned about introducing the cats and worried that they wouldn't get along. Also, one of her fiancé's cats was known to be territorial about her house. She barely tolerated his second cat and really became aggressive when she saw other cats outside the picture window that overlooked the front yard.

In order to make sure the introduction went well, I asked Tanya to start now and not wait until after the wedding. I suggested that she communicate with her cat in detail about the impending first introduction to her fiancé's cats. I also had her explain what the long-term plans were, what she needed from her cat, and why this would be a good thing for her cat. In turn, I had her fiancé do the same with his cats to make sure they knew what to expect, how to handle it, and why it would be a good thing for everyone. They followed my advice, visualized the entire process working as they planned, took a calming breath, and proceeded with the introduction.

I asked Tanya to keep her cat in her crate during the initial introduction to the new house and new cats. I suggested she bring in her cat and put her in the living room while still in her crate, and that the other cats be kept elsewhere in the house at this point. This would give her cat a little while to get used to the new smells and energy of the house.

After a short time, I suggested that she slowly move her cat to each room while still in the crate, and still keep her separate from the other cats. Once her cat, still in her crate, seemed to have some degree of comfort with everything, I suggested that the other cats join them and be introduced.

I asked them to ensure that the initial greeting take place in a neutral zone like their garage or yard. Or, if they preferred, they could stage the introduction in a room that wasn't often frequented by her fiancé's cats. It was best to allow her fiancé's cats to investigate Tanya's cat while she remained in her crate. I also asked them to make the first introduction of the cats brief, holding it to ten minutes, which would allow enough time for them all to smell one another's scent and feel one another's energy. Once the ten minutes had passed, I suggested that she praise her cat, provide her with a few special treats or food to reinforce how great a job she had done, and then drive home. In turn, I suggested her fiancé also reward his two cats and then go back in the house.

Every day for a week they followed this program, each day increasing the length of time the cats spent together. After a week had passed, I suggested they allow Tanya's cat to come out of her crate within a neutral area secured by a baby gate, with the other cats on the opposite side of the gate. This would allow all the cats their own space for a time, while still being able to see, hear, and smell one another and also feel one another's energy.

After a couple of weeks and no signs of aggression by any of the cats, I suggested they remove the baby gate and allow direct contact between all the cats. They followed my instructions, and the cats all got along splendidly. At first they were cautious and would just sit or lie on opposite ends of the room, away from one another. Eventually they moved closer, and within a few days they were sharing food dishes and favorite sleeping spots and sunbathing near the picture window. The staged approach worked, and all was well in their new home together.

## Tips for Introducing a New Dog or Cat into the Home

When introducing a new animal into the home, be sure to:

- Communicate with your present animals about what is going to happen, what you need from them, and why they will enjoy the new furry family member.
- Visualize the process going smoothly and with the outcome you expect.
- Introduce the animals in an outdoor or neutral location, not in the main house.
- Spend up to an hour in the outdoor or neutral location before moving to another area or the main section of the house.
- Based on how well things are progressing, stage the introduction of dogs over a few hours or over multiple days and the introduction of cats over a few days or a couple of weeks.

While bringing a new animal into your household may be stressful at first and you may wonder whether you've made the right decision, remember to be patient and remain calm and confident that all will turn out well. You will know intuitively and by the way the animals respond if the addition of a particular new animal is going to be a good fit for your family. If it's clear that a certain dog or cat is not going to be a good fit in the long run, it's better to know now than to spend a lifetime dealing with added confrontation. The new animal also deserves to be happy and find their right and perfect forever home.

# 31

## Sharing Toys and Treats

If your home is at all like mine, your dogs and cats have many toys and all sorts of wonderful treats. But what happens when one of your furry children doesn't like to share their toys and treats?

My schnauzer Woody was notorious for hoarding every toy that came into the house. There were literally hundreds of toys spread out in multiple doggy toy boxes and wicker baskets on each floor of our house. I used to travel a lot for business, and I'd keep a bag full of toys and treats in my car. Returning home from the airport, I would park my car in the garage and open the door to the house, where Buzz and Woody would be waiting for me. Their greetings were always world-class, and I knew they were glad I was home! They would stand on their two hind legs, give me hugs, and kiss me all over my face for several minutes. We then proceeded to the laundry room, where I would unzip my luggage. They waited in anticipation to see what I had brought home for them. I would open the front flap of the suitcase, and they would delicately nose through all my clothes to find the toys and treats hidden inside. Once they did, they would place them in their mouths and run to the living room to check out their latest surprises.

I always placed two of everything inside the suitcase so that each dog would have a toy or treat to take away. Though they each would find their respective toys and treats, Woody would always take Buzz's and try to keep it for himself. Buzz was always amenable to his brother's antics, but he would sit watching in disappointment. We knew we had to find a way to make sure Woody understood that this was not the way things were done in the household. So we communicated to Woody what he needed to do (let Buzz have his share of the toys and treats), why it would be a good thing (his brother would play more with the toys with him), and why it would make his brother and us extremely happy.

We decided to choose the keyword "share" with Woody in these situations. After the dogs would take the toys and treats into the living room, we would follow close behind. If Woody proceeded to hoard the new toys and treats, we would take the toys or treats from him and place them gently in front of each dog on their mat. We asked Woody to "share" the toys or treats. We then pointed toward the toys and treats and motioned for each of them to take just one. Woody would take the opportunity to be the first to select the toy or treat he wanted, and before long he started leaving the second toy or treat alone for his brother to enjoy. We would then praise them for doing such a good job and would spend quality time petting and playing with them and their new toys and treats.

We implemented this same strategy with our toy schnauzer,

Dusty, and our miniature schnauzer, Kramer. Dusty, always being the dog who likes to hoard her toys, needed to understand that there were plenty of toys to go around. We communicated with her that we needed her to "share" and be "gentle" with her "brother" when playing with the toys. Communicating this to her and using these keywords for these particular situations did the trick. Dusty is still young and needs frequent reminders, but we always go back to communicating with her and using our keywords. Doing so helps her understand that this is an all-the-time way of playing with toys, not just for when it suits her fancy.

Thankfully, our cats don't have a lot of challenges when it comes to sharing. They are grown now and show little interest in toys. They share their food and beds with one another on a regular basis. Only a few of the cats are treat motivated, with Ash, our gray tabby, being the main treat connoisseur. He loves his treats and never seems to get enough of the soft morsels that come out of the treat bag. He is front and center when he hears the bag crumple while I'm opening it. A few of the other cats will also come to investigate the bag when they hear the noise. This doesn't make Ash happy, often resulting in his hissing and swatting at them. In order to correct this undesirable behavior, we communicate with Ash. We let him know that there are plenty of treats to go around, and we use the keywords "be sweet" each time we go to give the cats treats. We place a few in front of Ash, say, "be sweet," and then proceed to give treats to the other cats. We then circle our attention back to Ash and place a few more in front of him to enjoy. We praise and pet him to acknowledge the great work he has just done and that he understood our keywords "be sweet."

## Tips to Encourage Sharing

I suggest following these steps when asking a dog or cat to share their toys or treats:

- COMMUNICATE AND VISUALIZE: Communicate verbally with your dogs and cats that they need to share their toys and treats. Visualize how you would like for them to receive the toys and treats. Explain to them that there are enough toys and treats for everyone.

- CHOOSE A KEYWORD OR WORDS: Choose a keyword or a couple of keywords that you specifically use in these situations. Use a word like "gentle" or "easy" to stress how you want them to handle the toy or act with each other when they receive a new toy or treat. Make sure the keyword or words are positive and only used in these situations.

- LET THE ALPHA RULE: It's okay to let the dog or cat who is perceived to be "the boss" of the group have the first selection; just make sure they share. Letting them choose first will make them feel like they are still in control of the situation and preclude any anxiety that would result if the "natural order" of their being in charge were disrupted.

- PRAISE: Once they have received their new toys and treats and have followed your instructions, be sure to praise all of them. This is especially true for the more demanding dog or cat. Let them all know they did a great job in sharing their toys and treats.

Sharing everything and treating all dogs or cats as equals are important in a group dynamic. It's no fun for anyone if the dogs and cats are fighting over every toy or treat. Following this process will allow everyone to understand the importance of sharing and should lead to fewer confrontations between the animals. It will also help prevent your dogs and cats from destroying their toys — and the resulting stuffing from being strewn all over the house.

# Afterword

After completing this book and rereading every word, sentence, and chapter many times, I'll admit that I feel great about the information I've shared with you. It's not only because I was able to share my message with you or that you chose to spend your time reading the book. I'm more pleased with the fact that you now have additional tools to better understand and communicate with your dogs and cats. Perhaps you will implement these steps and tools as part of your daily life with your dogs and cats. If what I've written resonates with you, then I'm thrilled. If it helps you build the best relationship possible with your dogs and cats, then I'm humbled to have been a part of it in some small way.

I've had the pleasure of being a professional animal communicator and consultant for more than a decade. I've worked with clients from around the world who have lost animals and looked for my guidance in finding and being reunited with their animals.

I've worked with families whose animals were preparing to make their transition from this world or had already passed on. They've looked to me to help them make the best decisions for the pets before their passing and to help with the grieving process afterward.

I've worked with other families whose animals have experienced a sudden change in behavior. They've sought my assistance to help them better understand the reasons why and to help correct the challenges their animals were facing.

Each and every situation is as unique as the animal involved. However, the steps and tools I use are the same ones that I have discussed in this book. I hope these steps and tools will help you better understand and communicate with all animals, especially your dogs and cats.

# Acknowledgments

I'm forever grateful for the love and support of my wonderful wife, Kim. She has been front and center from the beginning of my journey with the animals and has walked alongside me every step of the way. Her love of all animals is never-ending and she has taught me so much. Her ability to keep me focused while writing this book and her willingness to spend hours helping me edit the work haven't gone unnoticed. She is my biggest fan, my "rock" (for all the support she provides), and the inspiration in all that I do. I am truly blessed to have Kim as my wife.

I give my sincere and heartfelt appreciation to Victoria Stilwell for writing the foreword to this book. Her passion in standing up for animals is unmatched. Her continued support of me and the work I do is unwavering. I am so humbled by all that she has done for me. I am proud to have her as my friend.

I want to send a special thank-you to all the brilliant and talented people who have endorsed this book. Your kind words regarding my book and the work I do for animals have touched my heart.

I give much appreciation to Georgia Hughes, New World Library's editorial director, for believing in me and this project. She is a true professional and a joy to work with. I will be forever grateful for everything she has done.

I give thanks to the entire New World Library team. I give special thanks to Munro Magruder, marketing director and associate publisher; Monique Muhlenkamp, publicity director; Vicki Kuskowski, cover designer; Tona Pearce Myers, type designer; Jonathan Wichmann, assistant editor; and Kristen Cashman, managing editor. It's been an honor to work with such an outstanding team.

I am grateful to my entire dog and cat family, past and present: Woody, Buzz, Dusty, Kramer, Momma Kitty, Rusty, Natasha, Ash, Neecie, Bandit, and Baby. Each of you has been a bundle of unconditional love and joy and by far the best teachers I have ever had.

And last but certainly not least, I thank God for blessing me with so many gifts that allow me to assist in providing animals a voice.

# Recommended Reading and Supplemental Material

## Books

Link, Tim. *Wagging Tales: Every Animal Has a Tale.* Austin: Emerald Book Company, 2009.

Stilwell, Victoria. *It's Me or the Dog: How to Have the Perfect Pet.* New York: Hachette, 2007.

————. *Train Your Dog Positively: Understand Your Dog and Solve Common Behavior Problems Including Separation Anxiety, Excessive Barking, Aggression, Housetraining, Leash Pulling, and More.* New York: Ten Speed Press, 2013.

## On-Demand Audio Workshop

Link, Tim. *Learning to Communicate with Animals with Tim Link.* Pet Life Radio Productions, LLC, 2013. MP3.

# About the Author

Tim Link is the host of the nationally syndicated radio show *Animal Writes*, which airs on Pet Life Radio and iHeart Radio. He is also the author of *Wagging Tales: Every Animal Has a Tale* and a regular contributing writer for Victoria Stilwell's *Positively* pet expert blog and *Dogster* and *Catster* magazines.

Tim is a national speaker and has appeared as a guest on television and radio as well as in print media as an internationally recognized animal expert, communicator, and consultant.

Tim consults with families about their pets to resolve behavioral, emotional, and/or physical concerns. He also provides families with grief support when a pet has passed on or is in the process of passing on. In addition, Tim has received international recognition for his work locating missing animals.

As part of his ongoing mission to help animals, Tim has also mastered Reiki — an ancient art of energy healing — which he uses on animals to identify where physical or emotional problems may exist. For over a decade, Tim has helped many animals in many situations, and he continues to do so daily. He enjoys spending time with his wife, Kim, and their many pets at their home outside of Atlanta, Georgia.

For more information about Tim
and the services he provides, visit his websites,
www.wagging-tales.com or www.talkingwithdogsandcats.com,
or email him at timlink@wagging-tales.com.

Made in the USA
Lexington, KY
23 October 2016